To Herbert Krotchman
in appreciation of past
encouragement.

John F. Buchanan

D1488275

ANTIQUES AND COLLECTIBLE HUMOR

by

John F. Buchanan

A Hearthstone Book

Carlton Press, Inc.   New York, N.Y.

DEDICATION

To My Wife

ACKNOWLEDGMENTS

DON JOHNSON, Editor, *Antique Week,* Leesburg, VA. His agreeing to print two of my essays encouraged me to attempt a book.
HERBERT KRATCHMAN, Publisher, *Renninger's Antique Guide,* Lafayette Hill, PA. His publishing of two of my essays reinforced my thoughts of a compilation of stories.
LINDA SHANNON ROOF, an Art Teacher at Lackey High School, Charles County, MD. Her work on suggestions for illustrations is appreciated.
MY FAMILY, for their patience with me over the years.

JOHN BUCHANAN

PREFACE

Never say no!—I can't do that! That's the way we look at life. One evening, back in 1980, when chatting around the dinner table after a satisfying meal, one of our sons and his wife, our daughter, John and I were talking about what things we might do in the future.

I said, "After I leave the education business, (school administration), I'd like to have a little antique shop and I would call it "Buchanan's Bounty". Everyone agreed that would be interesting; end of conversation.

Several months later the phone rang and the female voice on the other end informed me that our small shop would be vacant and we could open for business on Labor Day. I informed her she had the wrong number. After exchanging pertinent information, I realized that my husband and son, had indeed gone to an antique center in the county and put our name on the list for a small shop. Talk about never say no!

After hanging up, questioning my husband's sanity, and having another cup of coffee I began to think, why not? Never mind that we had no experience with running a business, nor that the antique business was in a recession and we didn't have any stock. Suddenly, it seemed the thing to do.

My personal experience with antiques came from attending country auctions as a child with my father and being a Victorian buff. My Mother always referred to antiques and collectibles as junk and used furniture. What my father brought home, my mother threw out the back door, except for a cow and a pump organ. She continued this practice which included some of our possessions we intrusted to her care while we were stationed overseas. Needless to say, she didn't show much enthusiasm for our new venture.

All of a sudden, "Adventures in Antiqueland" were in full

swing. As you can see in my husband's book, it was a new experience, to say the least.

We have learned a lot in the last ten years. We've made silly mistakes, stumbled into fantastic buys and even made a little money but most of all we cherish the wonderful friendships we've made with other dealers, show managers and customers.

Right now we are in hiatus—the house and storage buildings are stuffed with stock—who knows what's next? But this we do know—we are—will have been—we will be a part of the antique world—wouldn't have missed it for anything!

ADALINE BUCHANAN

CONTENTS

Antique Humor—European Style 11
How to Furnish your Apartment or Home—European Style 14
Opening Day—in a Hurry 18
The Innocent Customer—The Innocent Dealer 21
The Captured Customers 24
Branching Out—Through Walls and Doors 29
Strange Acquisitions 33
Strange Merchandise 36
Antique Associations—A Hindrance or a Help 40
The Art of Buying 42
Shopping—The Tennessee Connection 47
Shopping—The Pennsylvania Connection 52
Shopping—The Ohio—West Virginia Connection 55
Here They Come—Two By Two's (or Three's) 58
The Two By Two's (or Three by Three's)—in Sync 62
Pete—The Watchcat 65
The Pause That Refreshes and Educates 70
More Show News—Never Published 73
The Auction—A Mystery to the Untutored 78
Reproductions—To Have Them or Have Them Not 81
The Street Show—A Fun Thing 84

Show News—Never Published 87

Moving In—The Joy of It 90

Moving Out—Another Joy 94

Deliveries—The Fun and the Backaches 98

Packing and Moving—A Collateral Trade 101

The Mystery of the Isolated Show 107

Gains and Losses—The Antique Equation 110

Old Movies and Plays—Antique Research 112

Management—A New Ball of Twine 116

Management and Advertising—More Education 120

Management and Maintenance 122

A Brief Sayonara—No More Playing House 125

ANTIQUES AND
COLLECTIBLE HUMOR

ANTIQUE HUMOR—EUROPEAN STYLE

The first collector from our family was my wife, Adaline. I was a soldier stationed in Europe and my hours on duty were unpredictable. Sometimes when I was away for a couple of days, she shopped at various places and started a small antique collection. While on these shopping expeditions, she discovered Waltzek's Antiques, a business located in Bad Nauheim, West Germany, a suburb of Frankfurt—a—Main. The first time my wife enticed me there, I saw a large warehouse filled with discarded furniture and glass. Antique dealers are people with perception and my wife could see beyond the awesome waste and imagine the beauty of a fine item, when restored to its proper state.

The experience of antiquing was interesting to me because it went beyond looking for a new restaurant, a good book or a new pair of shoes. When I had the time, I shopped with my wife and became very interested in old paintings. I hadn't taken any leave for some time and my wife suggested we travel to Belgium and see some of the places where I had been during World War II. On our first day, we tried to register at a rather plush hotel in Brussels but were refused because we had our little Pekingese, "Satch", with us.

Animals were not permitted in the hotel. We found an inexpensive pension halfway between Brussels and Antwerp, where we took nice rooms for a pittance. Satch was accommodated as well and when dinner was served, "Satch" was served with us.

The next day we wandered into an artist's show in Antwerp where we found a beautiful still-life of roses; it is still displayed in our home. We also found a nice painting of an Antwerp street scene. We have had some tempting offers to buy them by friends and customers, but we keep them because "Ole Satch" saved us the money with which we purchased them. The manager of the hotel in Brussels did his job, but we are the people grinning.

11

This is one of the paintings from Antwerp, Belgium, that "Ole Satch" helped us buy in 1956.

A friend of mine with whom I had been stationed in Korea arrived in Bad Kissingen, Germany, and invited us to visit and meet his family. Upon arrival, my son immediately sold his son a shooting marble at a reasonable price. "Another antique dealer on the horizon, no doubt", said my friend.

Paul, my friend, and his wife were rearing four children in an adequate military apartment. In addition to the living occupants of this home were seven German grandfather clocks which he had procured at very good prices. His aim was to ship them back to the United States and sell them at a great profit.

We had trouble sleeping that first night as the clocks chimed on the hour and half-hour and not necessarily at the same time. My friend said later on that he had disconnected the chimes on all the clocks but one, but not on the night we were there. We visited from time to time and corresponded when he returned to the States. Some years later I asked him how much he had profited from his clocks. He lowered his eyes and said, "Not much. When we came home, everybody had one and most of them were just like mine. We also exceeded our shipping allowance and had to pay the difference." I told him my wife had shipped a rock from the Swiss Alps with our things and they didn't charge us a penny extra. He didn't laugh.

There are times when humor results from a sincere effort to restore something to its original beauty. I was surprised when I returned home from work one Saturday to find a pile of utter trash on the parlor floor. There was a pile of wood, rusty springs, rotting cord and webbing which had once been Victorian chairs. My tired body and mind told me, "She's been to Waltzeck's again but this time she's gone too far!" After some food and rest, we went to the library and found a book on the restoration of old furniture. The more we read, the more interesting the project of restoration became.

We pulled the five hundred little upholstery tacks from the hard wood, filled the holes with wood putty, wiped the wood clean and then glued and repaired most of the damage; thence to some finer refinishing. I researched cleaning the springs, taking off the old ties and making new ones. My wife then researched the reupholstering process and applied the new webbing. When I read the part about installing the springs, things started to get funny. REAL FUNNY! "You mean after making all these ties, (six on each spring and then secured to the others), I have to sit on a board to depress them and fasten them to the base of the chair before I can get back on my feet?", I asked. My wife answered, "Just like the book says, but think of the accomplishment; the rest will be a piece of cake."

We ignored our project for a week or so, and finally I was inspired to continue my part. The job was laborious, to say the least. To secure the ties with hammer and tacks, with your head inclined, sitting on a board and trying to breathe normally was not an every day process. While I was about this task, a knock came at the door and our neighbor from across the hall in the apartment building arrived for a visit. "Hi, John", she greeted, "How are you doing and what are you doing?" "Oh, not much," I answered, "just a little busy right now; talk to you later."

Our friend, Mary, and Adaline went into the kitchen. My children had returned from school and stood by in amazement as I labored. When Mary and my wife came back into the parlor, Mary asked, "What is John doing with his head between his knees, all red in the face, cursing and sitting on that chair? Has he been drinking?" My wife answered, "No, he's putting the springs back in that old chair." Mary gave us both a slow stare and remarked, "Of course, of course", and left us.

Regardless of Mary's evaluation of what I was doing, we grinned about it a few years later when we sold those two chairs.

HOW TO FURNISH YOUR APARTMENT OR HOME—EUROPEAN STYLE

We started the process of furnishing our future home in Europe. At that time, we were occupying Army temporary quarters and the basic furnishings were three children and two Pekingese dogs. The Pekes were white, very rare in Europe, and the Europeans, Germans in particular, were wild about them and some offered a lot of money for them. We considered them family property, not for sale. No one even considered buying our children; of course, they weren't for sale either. We also had a few comfort items that we had shipped from the U.S. About this time, 1966, we moved into these temporary quarters in Frankfurt, West Germany, located on the fifth floor of the apartment complex.

The top floor used to be maids' quarters in the early days of the American occupation but now the maids no longer lived in the complex, thus they were used for "temps", as they were called. The "temp" consisted of a living room, shower and bath, a very small kitchen and seven small bedrooms. This allowed for plenty of room for antiques and collectibles after we started to look for them. My wife and I had the luxury of a dressing room across from our bedroom. The children had a ball, using the extra rooms at their discretion. The people who lived on the fourth floor had only one request. "Don't let the kids roller-skate up there, like the last family. It sounds like an artillery barrage down there", they told us. I assured them we would honor their request.

We told our friends later that this was our Greenwich Village apartment in Germany. These quarters offered great exercise opportunities as well, especially when carrying eight or ten sacks of groceries from the car up to the kitchen.

One humorous situation arose from this high altitude environment. The temporary quarters had slanting roofs; thus when I shaved, I had to tilt my head. After we moved to permanent-type quarters, about four months later, it took me about two weeks to cease from tilting my head when I shaved. All in all, we enjoyed living up there in the rafters and were sort of sad when the time came to move. We especially enjoyed watching the fireworks from up there on New Year's day of 1966.

15

During this time we used to go to the Officers' Club in Frankfurt now and then for dinner. One Sunday an antique dealer from Mainz, Germany, had a display in the large parlor-type entrance. We liked his display and picked up one of his cards with directions to his shop. A couple of weeks later, we traveled there and acquired a large, six-foot pier mirror with a marble topped console table. It was a beautiful item but weighed a ton. It had originated in Kiev, Germany. These were separate items, as the mirror had to be hung and the wall table secured eight feet and two inches below it. Later, when the men delivered it, they began to curse on the third floor and were downright "going up in flames" by the time they reached the fifth floor. When permanent quarters were available, we were fortunate in moving to the first floor in the same building.

The men who moved us developed the same attitude toward the mirror and table as had their predecessors. They said some things in German that we did not understand but considering the expressions on their faces, it was just as well we did not comprehend them. I had a half case of beer and some partially filled liquor bottles which I offered them and so they left, after their labors, in a happy mood and singing German marching songs.

Other items gradually came into our overseas home. My wife found some Austrian tier curtains for our large picture window. They looked just as nice from the outside balcony as from the inside sitting room. She found a marvelous Russian piece; a boat shaped bowl, silver plate on copper with a cut glass insert. We still have it. Later, a table and chairs came along and soon most of the Army furnishings had been taken back to the Quartermaster warehouse. When our friends visited they would remark, "This place doesn't even look like an Army apartment. Your furnishings must have cost a lot of money!" "Not really", my wife would reply. "I'm a 'junker', a person who shops the second hand shops. Have you picked up any European items since you've been here?" One lady answered, "Absolutely nothing so far. All I have now is Early Quartermaster."

Other acquisitions were a French kidney shaped desk for a lady, hand carved and beautiful and a folding felt lined card table with rotating top. The Europeans made a multitude of rotating and folding tops for tables, to preserve space in their apartments.

Probably the oldest antique we have is a French kitchen table, very heavy with a folding and rotating top which we used almost thirty five years and still is going strong. Circa late 1700's. We served our meals, plus three children and many guests during that time. Adaline says, "Any table, regardless of when it was made, that would survive our three children, their friends and ours, must certainly have been created by a great craftsman."

After two years in Frankfurt, I was transferred to Mannheim, Germany, a one day move. The furniture was loaded and moved to Mannheim in one day and we drove the forty-five mile trip the following morning. The Quartermaster people there were amazed at the amount of furniture they had to move out and the amount of our own they had to move in, but by dinner time we were set up and the apartment looked just like the one in Frankfurt. It took a couple of days to realize we had moved at all.

My wife had always considered Heidelberg, Germany, her favorite city and here we were, just fifteen minutes away. "I can't wait to go shopping over there", she said. Military wives are not usually happy about moving but she was overjoyed! Naturally, she acquired some "goodies" on her many trips to Heidelberg and we enjoyed the good restaurants that were in abundance.

The two best items were found in a rather shoddy place in Mannheim. They were large early Victorian walnut sofas. An elderly upholsterer in Heidelberg converted them to things of beauty.

His work was perfection and striking to the eye. "It would be sacrilege to sit on them", a neighbor said, but we and our guests sat on them as many did through the years, and enjoyed them. We kept them in our home for many years, twenty-five in fact, and finally sold them to make way for newly found things.

The great mirror from Kiev stands at the top of the stairway, the French desk is in the parlor and the old French kitchen table is still in our kitchen. These and some American antiques furnish our permanent home.

Even the dog is an antique. Experts say one year of human life is equal to seven years in a dog's life. I believe this equation is true because it takes me about as long to get out of a comfortable chair as it takes the dog to get up off the floor and on his feet. When we take a walk, we don't go as fast as we once did and his moans and groans come from the same areas as mine; the legs

and back. But we're good friends. The dog figures we've known each other about seventy-five years now.

OPENING DAY—IN A HURRY

We had a fairly extensive collection of antiques that we had gathered together from the nineteen-fifties to the eighties. In fact, the house and storage shed were becoming a bit cluttered. My wife was still teaching but I wasn't very busy at the time, so my son, who is always on the lookout for ways to make a little extra money said to me, "You and Mom ought to start an antique shop. You have enough merchandise now; you wouldn't even have to go shopping."

Later in the day my son kept nudging me about a shop, so to ease the chatter for awhile, we drove to an antique complex some six miles away called "Peddlers Paradise". We looked around a bit and then approached the managers of the complex at that time, a nice elderly couple. They had run this antique center for some ten years. We asked about renting a shop and were informed that there were no vacancies at that time, but we would be placed on a waiting list. I still had reservations about all this and hoped the waiting list was long or that the managers would forget about us. My son still badgered me, "Put your name on the list. You'll have time between now and when they call to think about it." I did so and it was done; the beginning of a fascinating experience.

We were surprised when two weeks later, two rooms at the complex became available. My wife and I talked with the managers the following weekend concerning the pluses of and minuses of operating in the antique center. Some of the minuses were offset by very reasonable rent.

Some of the minuses not offset were freezing in winter, roasting in summer, and a complete restoration of the two rooms in record time. We also had a restroom that didn't work.

This was the seventeenth of September, 1980, and we had just a few days to fix the place up and open on the first of the next month when the rent became payable. My wife, who likes to preserve a "buck" as much as my son likes to procure one said, "We're going to have to hurry, hurry to get in on time." "What's the hurry?", I asked. I should have known the answer which was, "You don't think we're going to pay rent for something we're not using, do you?" Hi Ho! Hi Ho!! And it was off to work we went. There was a lot to be done. The previous occupant of these two rooms had dealt in glassware and china, therefore, our first job was to pull about two thousand nails from the walls before we could paint. The place had to be cleaned, the windows washed and the floor painted. To save time, we merely painted the borders of the floor and laid some rugs down. Then, of course, the merchandise had to be moved in and if we had not had the help of my son and his wife, we would not have made the deadline. We are still grateful to them and my daughter, who helped also.

On opening day, amateurs that we were, we discovered we had forgotten something. We had brought too much merchandise.

Guess what we had forgotten? Shelves for one thing and in addition a Trader's License, a requirement in Maryland. We found you either had to have shelves installed, or build them.

I built them and they passed, after being painted. My son's wife made some flower arrangements to help decorate the place and her hard work in helping us prepare the shop, provided her with a surprise. Some of the first items to be sold in the shop were her flower arrangements.

An incident happened during the opening process that made me look stupid. Everyone else though it was funny. We had an overhead light in both rooms which provided minimal lighting so we took several lamps, both floor and table types to the shop. After hooking them up, they would not light. I had used several extension cords and thought this might be the problem but after many pluggings and unpluggings, they still would not function. I finally approached the manager. He called the "Jack-Of-All-Trades" who kept this old edifice in original but operable status. The building, as a matter of fact, had been a motel at one time. This being a weekend, the man was hard to locate but he finally appeared in our shop on Sunday afternoon. "What's the problem?", he asked. I told him the lamps would not come on and we badly needed them.

He walked to the switch near the front door of the first room and flipped it on. All the lamps came on and I felt like I was standing naked with a spot light trained on me. The electrician looked at me in a strange way. I'm glad my son wasn't there. He'd still be laughing. The "Jack-Of-All Trades" said, "You see, this is an old motel and all the plugins are hooked to the room switch".

The managers told us to watch our first customers very carefully as the "pick up" artists like to prey on people just starting a new shop. The lady manager told my daughter to be especially watchful of women carrying large shopping bags. We had good surveillance from the door between the rooms and I really wasn't concerned about theft, but my daughter took this warning very seriously.

She actually started following customers around the shop and not knowing her, they considered her another shopper. After the first weekend she said at Sunday dinner, "This shop business is sort of fun but I nearly walked myself to death this weekend." I advised her to follow groups of customers or every other customer to cut down on the mileage, if she was still inclined to do this sort of thing. We had remarkable luck through the years. One day someone took a small needle holder from one of the phonographs which was worth about five cents. If the person who lifted it would have asked for it, I would have given it to him.

Our first weekend was a slow one with little intake. My wife said it reminded her of an antique dealer near our hometown in Ohio. She used to say, "Most antique dealers buy and sell. I just buy." My son said he appreciated my asking him to become a partner, but right now, not seeing any "bucks" coming in, he would just observe the business. He further jabbed at me. "I don't think your bookkeeping will keep you up late at night."

A friendly dealer told me not to worry, because at the end of our first year, everything in those two rooms would be gone. I asked, "Will you buy everything left over at the end of the year?" He answered in the negative as his faith was not as firm as his prediction. But, we did well. When things started to look up financially, my son expressed his desire to take my offer of partnership. I told him to keep observing for awhile.

THE INNOCENT CUSTOMER—THE INNOCENT DEALER

When my wife and I started doing antique shows, we sometimes were depressed when we came away the losers; the same attitude prevailed after a slow week at our shop.

After observing the real professional antique dealers accept a loss with dignity, we adjusted our behavior accordingly. We learned by observations that if you don't want to gamble, don't play the game. On slow days at our shop, or during a lull in the activity of a show, some marvelous stories unfold which reinforce the dealers' attitude, patience and amiable outlook.

On a slow day at our shop, when walking around a corner from another room, my heart skipped a beat when I saw a very large lady trying to sit on one of our tiny gout stools. The stool's little legs were quivering and straining to support the stress being applied by this lady's weight.

The gout stool was developed in the old days to support the

painfully throbbing and swollen foot of the patient. The stool was padded and shaped in a "V" form, and supported by four tiny legs; sometimes the legs were fitted with casters. The stool was designed to support the calf of the leg and relieve the pressure on the afflicted foot. This was one of the early applications of relief of the victim, before modern medicine prescribed a pharmaceutical method of releasing the poison from the system which caused the illness and severe pain.

I helped the good lady, who appeared to have difficulty rising to her feet, and she looked with disdain upon my gout stool. She said, "It's a cute little stool but sits awful low to the floor."

After I had explained the intended use of the stool and the history of it, she began to show more interest. I explained to her that it was a reproduction but a good one, made by a young man in Ohio, whose great-granddad, granddad, father and now he had been crafting for generations. She then had a little laugh on herself and cheerfully bought one in good condition. Thus a laugh saved the day for both of us.

One of my neighboring dealers called me to help her arrive at a fair price for an article of glassware. As I walked into her shop, she was with a young couple admiring a hoosier cabinet. It was a nice one and had been on the floor of her shop for some time. As the young couple were opening doors and examining the several compartments, the wife said, "Honey, I've always wanted one like this with an ice crusher inside." I retreated to my shop to enjoy a private chuckle. My friend explained the use of the flour sifter to the young lady and after a laugh together, the hoosier cabinet was sold. Laughter had saved the day once more.

Our complex contains fifteen shops, all managed by individual dealers. The building is an old motel which has been reorganized to accommodate shops.

There is a nice lawn in front upon which is erected a huge billboard type sign which reads, "PEDDLERS PARADISE, ANTIQUES". After dusk the sign is illuminated with spotlights and even a person with poor vision could see it a quarter of a mile away. One Sunday, a rather slow day, my wife was sitting in a folding chair in front of our shop, reading a book. Two ladies, who appeared to be mother and daughter, left their car and discussed their plan for shopping. The daughter went to the North end of the complex and the mother entered our shop, spent some time looking at the merchandise, returned to the front and met her daughter coming back from the North end. The daughter asked, "Anything interesting in there?" The mother answered, "No, nothing in there but antiques." So much for our huge sign, so much for advertising but a lot to say for a good story which most people laugh about, particularly antique dealers.

A memorable day in our antique business came about when I sold my wife's replica of a famous race horse with the jockey mounted atop. She had taken it to our shop to use as a doorstop and it worked beautifully. A dealer from North Carolina, with a sharp eye, offered to buy it at what I thought was a reasonable price. The price was reasonable; very, very reasonable. She paid for it and probably giggled all the way to Durham, where the "Bulls" have a baseball team, or wherever she hailed from down that way. A few days later my wife discovered the horse and jockey missing and inquired as to their whereabouts.

I told her I had sold it at a "good" price and when I told her the "good" price she turned pale. She then exhibited some of the talent she had developed in the years when she taught high school physical education. Considering her advanced age, I was astonished by the way she could jump up at least two feet in the air, flail her arms and at the same time loudly question my ancestry. This item had been a gift from her father after her graduation from high school. He owned race horses and this brass one was a replica of a Maryland champion. The jockey was considered a great one in his time.

I blamed it all on her because she had not told me its history but she has yet to accept my excuse. The lady in North Carolina is laughing, I am crying and my wife still has the incident locked between her ears. Through the yeas I sometimes chuckle about it, but my wife has yet to see any humor connected with the matter. If anyone who reads this ever visits our shop, please don't remind her of it. Thank you.

THE CAPTURED CUSTOMERS

After I retired from the U.S. Army and my wife had retired as a High School Principal, we entered the antique world, operating a shop and doing antique shows. We found the business interesting and rewarding. During the past ten years some humorous incidents have occurred and I have made note of them because I feel they are worth remembering.

One situation arose at a recent show that surprised me, but the more I thought about it, the funnier it became. We had an extensive display at the show and had taken most of the "set up" day to arrange our merchandise. We had taken classical furniture, some nice glass and paintings along with two phonographs which were in excellent condition. We also displayed a large server, a platform rocker and two marble-top tables.

The "show pieces" or center of attraction was a seven piece set of Renaissance furniture including four chairs. A customer came to me and asked about "the price of your chair?" After explaining

that the chairs were part of a seven piece set, she remarked, "No, not those." I continued, "Then you must be interested in the platform rocker." She then said, "No, I mean the one you were sitting on." It was a wooden folding chair, furnished by the promoter, two each, to all dealers. I referred her to the promoter who perhaps sold her a chair. Sometimes we show the wrong merchandise.

At one time, we had an antique wicker baby carriage with metal wheels, along with brake and an adjustable hood. These were popular in the 1920's, at least I think they were, as I have a picture of my mother pushing me around in one. This one was in remarkable condition for its age and made an attractive display in our shop. At the same time, my son and his wife were parents of a year old baby girl. They always had the baby with them, including their visits to our shop. On a particular Sunday they visited and asked me to watch the baby while they looked through some of the other shops. While they were gone, the baby became sleepy so I put some padding and a blanket in the carriage and she quietly slept. Meanwhile, I tried to accommodate the customers passing through the shop.

A young couple admired the carriage and I gave them information about the age, etc. They particularly liked the adjustable hood which could be moved to shade the baby's eyes. They left a deposit for it and said they would be back when they had completed their shopping. When they returned we had another discussion concerning price and I wondered why they debated about the original agreement. Then the young woman said, "Where is the beautiful doll that went with the carriage?" I told her the "doll" was very much alive and with her parents. I sold the carriage for a lesser price but an innocent child had unknowingly made her first antique sale. Motto: Think about price before putting a live baby in an antique carriage.

On vacation a few years ago, we drove to Lewes, Delaware, a small, quiet bayside village. We vowed that we would not "antique" but rather sun, swim, fish and enjoy some good seafood. We were only halfway to Lewes, when we sighted a Baptist Church yard sale. Then we broke our vow. Of all things, we purchased a stuffed fox. Why would one want a stuffed fox?

In the four days we were in Lewes, we visited about twenty antique shops, numerous outside markets, one major show in

26

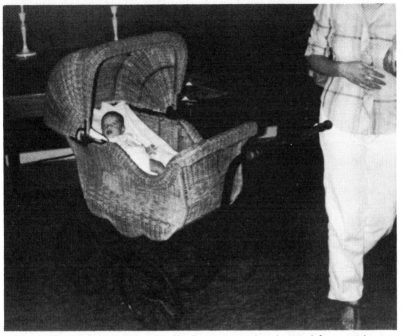

Our granddaughter, Jennifer Buchanan, resting in a wicker carriage.

Rehoboth Beach, Delaware, and three auctions. We had violated all our vows and returned home with a full station wagon plus items we lashed to the top of the vehicle. We packed the stuffed fox in the rear of the wagon and it stared viciously at the startled occupants of the cars which followed us. I remarked to my wife, "I think I have a low tire or the rear wheel is about to fall off because everyone behind us have a concerned expression on their faces." I eased the wagon to the side of the road and we walked back to examine the rear wheels. The fox glared at us from the back window. The taxidermist had done an excellent job; even the teeth shown from the partially open mouth. My wife said, "Move the fox and the enchantment from those following us will cease."

We kept it at home in the den until my daughter returned home at a late hour and switched the wall lamp on. She screamed so loudly it woke me from a deep sleep. She was happy when we took it to our shop for sale; so was my dog as he had circled it for three days before deciding the fox might be too much for him and did not attack.

Fate must have programmed me for the strange and funny things that occur in the antique business. One incident I shall remember eternally happened on a hot July afternoon. Three ladies from Massachusetts walked through the shop and we chatted about the merchandise. These nice ladies spoke with the clipped Northeastern accent that I enjoy hearing. They browsed about thirty minutes and departed. Another customer entered and when he left I locked the front and back doors and drove home as it was then six o'clock in the evening.

As I walked into the house, the phone rang. I answered and a female voice with a Northeastern accent asked, "Is Mr. Buchanan there?" I answered in the affirmative and the voice continued, "We are calling from your shop." There was a public telephone in our complex and I assumed she was calling from there. "Are you interested in seeing some of our merchandise again?", I asked. The voice retorted, "Listen, Mr. Buchanan, we are looking at your merchandise BECAUSE WE ARE IN YOUR SHOP! You left and LOCKED US IN HERE! You had better get back down here RIGHT NOW!"

I drove back to the shop nervously because I knew full well what to expect when I arrived. *HELL HATH NO FURY* like that of three women from Massachusetts locked in a strange antique shop in Maryland, a long way from home.

One of my neighboring dealer friends asked me later, "Did any sales result from this experience?" Funny man.

BRANCHING OUT—THROUGH WALLS AND DOORS

Six months after we started our business, two rooms next to ours became available and the managers gave us the first crack at them. We accepted as we did need more room. They were about the same size as our present ones and, again, they required work to prepare them for customers. Why people leave dirty, cluttered rooms behind, I do not know but this seems to be the pattern. There were shower rooms on both sides, this being an old motel building, and they had to be cleaned out first before the hard work began. We used them for storage rooms for extra merchandise.

The walls separating the two back rooms were simply two by fours covered with plaster-board, which was easily removed. This adjustment provided us with one large back room. There was a door separating the front rooms which had been sealed. I simply removed the door and we had entry into both front rooms. Then we painted, put down some more rugs, washed the windows and moved some merchandise, of which there was an abundance by now. It's amazing, once one has the antique bug, how much can be acquired in such a short period of time. We also gained another gas stove which we purchased from the departing dealer.

In one storeroom, (shower), I found about seventy-five old Playboy magazines which I thought would sell but didn't, however they provided good reading on slow days or browsing material for the husbands who stopped by with their wives and who could care less about antiques.

It was not long before two more rooms were available and when they were offered to us, we again accepted. I began to wonder why these other shops were failing but my wife advised me that the occupants merely had to move to other locations for business or family reasons.

The work was not so easy this time as I had to go through a

30

wall that was a main sustaining section. There was also electrical circuits running through this section, so I had to be careful where to plan the aperture for the door. The manager, being familiar with the building's structure, advised me where to work. This time, under the plaster was cinder block so I had to arm myself with a sledge hammer and a saw. I told my wife, "This time, I think we have gone a wall too far." An expert advised me that after you have blasted through the cinder block, a saw will cut through the rest and much to my astonishment, it worked. My daughter hauled the concrete waste away in a wheel barrow and immediately demanded a raise on her allowance. This was our last "branching out" and I was happy about it.

We now had two large gas stoves and one small one which we thought would be sufficient to heat the shop during the winter months. They didn't come close to doing the job. The wind came through that old motel building like it does in an aircraft testing tunnel. Trying to insulate the windows, we made the mistake of doing it with plastic cloth on the outside. It blew away like tissue paper the first time a strong wind came up. My wife had a lot of heavy curtains in storage and we put these up and they helped somewhat.

The next winter we wisely insulated the windows on the inside. Also, another dealer installed a kerosene stove which heated his shop nicely and naturally the other dealers, ourselves included, followed suit. We were finally warm but not for long. The owners were reminded by their insurance company that a clause in their contract prohibited the use of kerosene stoves. We were the only antique complex in the immediate area to have a kerosene stove sale.

We had reached the end of our efforts to be comfortable during the winter and just lived with the cold. One of our dealers had a line of long underwear and lumberjack shirts which he sold at reasonable prices and this winter his sales climbed up and up. I had a couple of sets of "longies" left over from Army days so my wife and I rescued them from a closet and avoided this additional overhead expense.

The winter had mercifully passed, and now we were faced with another adversary, the horsefly of summer. These were the large, bloodsucking variety that could drive people mad. Adaline told me we had to have screen doors. I remarked, "Since we now have

31

four front doors and four back doors, how many should I install?" "Four will be enough", she replied, "seal four doors and with the other four open, we will have a cross draft in the shop." I installed the screen doors but the customers kept closing the solid doors when they left the shop. People are funny. They close the doors in summertime and leave them open in winter. One of our dealers had to put hooks on the back of the doors to keep people from closing them.

We now had six shower, "(storage)" rooms which provided plenty of storage space. We had all our show equipment, lights, extension cords, easels, etc., in one room which made them easily accessible, when needed. The others were used for various things. Each time we had branched out, all the dealers came through to observe the changes which had taken place. One of the dealers, however, continued to wander through the shop at least once a week and persisted in looking through all the storage rooms. We thought this to be a bit strange if not downright "nosey". How were we to deal with this ill-mannered situation? One of our other dealer friends solved the problem for us. He had a skeleton in his shop which he had shoved back in a corner and practically forgotten. He and I, being practical joke oriented, devised a rig in one of the storerooms to discourage the "nosey one". We hung the skeleton from the ceiling and rigged it so that when the door was opened the light would come on, a spotlight, and one arm would rise in the air. It even scared me, the first time we tried it.

A couple of days later our inquisitive friend arrived and started her usual tour of the premises. A few minutes later I heard a blood-curdling scream. Our "nosey" one had happened upon our apparition. Soon she came barging into the room where I was working at my desk and demanded, "What are you doing, may I ask, with a skeleton in that closet!?" "What were you doing in the closet?, I asked. She had nothing more to say and departed. She didn't look into any of our storage rooms from that day forward.

My friend told me later she asked him where I had found the skeleton. He told her my daughter was taking a nursing course at the Community College and needed it to study anatomy. She accepted his answer. As a matter of fact, she hardly came in the shop at all but occasionally I would notice her looking through a window.

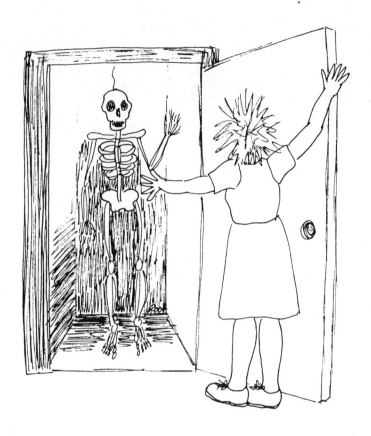

STRANGE ACQUISITIONS

As we shop in the antique world, either for our own possessions or for items for resale, we sometimes acquire merchandise that appears to be strange to others, if not in fact, truly strange to ourselves. We shop in Virginia frequently and on one occasion I noted a couple of unusual paintings, not so much for the settings but rather the procedure that was used in painting them. The scenes themselves were of the landscape variety. One was called the "Danube" and depicted a blueish colored river, a castle overlooking it, and a full moon shining over all. It was contained in an oval frame. The shop proprietor explained to me, "These were done by the artist on the back of glass in reverse form so we call them reverse paintings." The one of the Danube was quite old; another was of the White House in Washington, D.C., and its age was difficult to predict. I bought both of them and several others later on during our shopping tours. We still have two of these strange items. Our customers either liked them or didn't understand them, even after an explanation of the technique was made. One customer told me, "Reverse? Painted on the back side of glass in reverse? I don't believe it!" Another said they were "chipped and sloppy", discounting their age. Everyone has their preferences, I guess.

Unusual photographs sometimes move well or they attract attention to other merchandise surrounding them. One of the other dealers in our complex had a picture of four girls "stomping" grapes. I liked it and relieved her of it. The photo was taken, judging from the dresses the girls were wearing, during the late thirties or early forties. They had raised their skirts in order to stomp the grapes without soiling their clothing. For that day and age, they had their skirts raised to a height that was downright racy. We had no idea where the photo had been taken but one customer volunteered the information that there had been, during this era, a restaurant and night club in Washington, D.C., that had promoted such an event as "grape stomping" to bolster business. Another customer advised us that "This picture was taken in the wine country of Virginia. The winery conducted tours and as a part of the tour the visitors were given samples to taste. After a few tastes the girls were selected from the group to 'stomp the grapes' and pictures were taken." His story was as good as the first one as far as we were concerned. Finally, a gentleman passed through the shop, looked at the picture and immediately bought it. After the business transaction was over I asked him, "Do you know where that picture was taken?" He answered, "I not only know *where* it was taken, the last girl on the right is my wife! I DON'T LIKE IT HANGING AROUND IN SHOPS OR ANY OTHER PLACE! I now have four of them. If you see any more, let me know. OK?" The place the picture was taken was, in fact, the Virginia winery.

Another unusual picture is of our High School band taken from the top of the football stadium during the early 1940's. This was

Logan High School in Ohio and the band was formed in the "L.H.S." formation. I hadn't seen it for years and one day recovered it from a box of photos which had been stored in a closet. It brought back some pleasant memories and I was compelled to have it framed and hung it in our shop. Strangely enough it attracted a considerably amount of attention. Customers asked about it and I would explain the history of the picture. "I was a freshman when that taken", I would tell them. "And where are you in the picture?", they would ask and I would answer, "See that 'L' in the photo. Well, I'm standing there right behind that bass horn. You can't see me but I'm there." Some of the customers gave me a strange glance, probably wondering why a man would want a picture in which he couldn't see himself.

My wife returned home from shopping from time to time with strange items. One such item was an old bird cage. It was so differently made from the customary ones that I really didn't recognize it as such but, of course, it was disassembled as well. It was a large cage and stood about four feet high. After I had all the parts arranged I discovered it was two cages in one, one above the other. Each section had its own feeder, swing etc. We improved its appearance by painting it white. We didn't do so very well with it at first, and like all strange items, we had an interesting experience with it. My wife explained to a customer that this was a double-decker cage which could house two birds. The customer asked, "Why would anyone want a cage for two birds?" My wife told her the cage could be used to "sleep two birds or mate four." The customer gave her a funny look and departed.

One interesting item we came across was "Clarke's Fairy Light". These were little lamps which were proclaimed to produce a "safety lamp" which would burn for some nine hours. They were tiny, only about four inches in height and made with special glass. The bottom portion was white and the top was blue. They were so safe that they could be used in nurseries.

The Clarke Company manufactured a larger lamp, called "The Pyramid Night Light" and was proclaimed to reduce robberies at night. The advertisement read, "A Pyramid Night Light should be used in the front and back of every home, as soon as it is dark. The police recommend a Pyramid Night Light as the best safeguard. Almost all the burglaries perpetrated might have been prevented and much VALUABLE PROPERTY SAVED, if this simple and inexpensive plan had been adopted. Manufactured in Patent Fireproof Plaster Cases." An 1867 poem read:

When nights are dark, then think of Clarke,
Who's hit the nail precisely.
For his Night-Lights, Create light-nights,
In which you see quite nicely.—W.E.

If any of the readers need a "Fairy Lamp," we have one.

Back in the Victorian era, which was very naughty according to history, the bootjack was very popular. It was simply a device that the wearer could hook the end of his boot on and with considerable strength, pull it off his foot. There were two famous types; one a model of a cricket and the other was fashioned after a lady referred to as "Naughty Nellie". "Nellie was made of wrought iron and came in various sizes. The model depicted a lady, devoid of clothes and laying in a most compromising position. The gentleman placed the heel of his boot over the extended legs and pulled. These were extensively used in saloons, poolhalls, men's clubs and places that we can only describe here as illreputable. We acquired one and displayed it in our shop. One sedate lady customer told me, "You should be put in jail for having something like that in your shop!" I replied, "They better enlarge the jails because 'Ole Nellie' is all over this old world!"

The lady with the complaint had a husband who liked it and purchased the "Ole Nellie". Remarkably, the man's wife told mine, "I can't understand it. He's a Minister of The Gospel." When he appeared to pay for it, his gentle wife said, "You can have it, but put it in your antique collection, not mine."

STRANGE MERCHANDISE

Items of merchandise that are out of the ordinary or "strange", as some customers refer to them, are difficult to sell if you, the dealer, have no knowledge of their origin or history. One such item or items was a pair of Oriental gauntlets from India or China, according to the individual we purchased them from. It was hard to estimate their age. Being brass, they were very heavy, weighing about ten pounds each. The handwork and design on the outside was nicely done. They had a metal grip inside

and they fitted over the hand. A face had been carved on the front and the mouth was a slit through which a short knife could be used. There were little spikes all over the outside so that if the knife missed you could scratch a person considerably as an after effect. I absolutely guarantee that the first assailant able to strike the first blow was the winner. People were curious about them, but not enough so, to buy them. "Don't be discouraged", my wife said, "after all, this is not one of your everyday personal protection items." Finally, after giving the "gauntlet lecture" about five hundred times, a young lady bought them at a show in Delaware. She was a volunteer fire fighter and after her purchase we wondered if she were engaged in any other type of fighting. Possibly

37

she had a mean husband or it was rough around there on Saturday nights. If she did have trouble with someone, I'll bet she won!

As visitors and shoppers at a good show, we found a twelve piece dresser set made of celluloid. The sets usually consist of a comb, brush, button hook, mirror, fingernail file, etc. We were told that the manufacturers of this product discontinued it in the 1930's because celluloid was inflammable and considered to be a fire hazard, however we don't know if this is actually true. After we purchased it, and displayed it in our shop and at shows, it attracted a lot of attention, particularly among the young people. A lady shopper asked my wife on one occasion, "Why does that powder box have a hole in the top?" My wife explained that this was not a powder box but rather a hair receiver. Back in the 30's the women saved their "combings". Later, when they had a sufficient supply, they made "rats", literally stuffing for pompadors, a popular procedure in those days. Some people have preconcluded that antique dealers do not speak the truth. As the lady walked away, I heard her remark to her shopping companion, "Some of the stories they tell! That was a nice set and I would have bought it if that hole wasn't on the top of the powder box."

Sometimes, as dealers, we buy things that we feel doubtful about and we are quite positive that a mistake is in the making, but some strange compulsion overcomes our better judgement and we make the purchase anyway. An itinerant salesman passed through our shop one day and exhibited some small plastic boxes about two cubic inches in size with little flower designs on them. They came in a gross of one hundred and forty-four and the salesman's price was reasonable enough. I usually don't buy merchandise unless Adaline and I agree on the item, but she happened to be gone at the time.

We chatted awhile and he said, "Boy, it's hot in here! I could stand a cold one right about now!" "I just happen to have some in a cooler in the closet", I replied. We both had one or two and after the second one those little blue, purple, white and pink boxes began to look better to me. "I think I'll take a gross of them from you", I told him, "they'll make nice ring boxes or hold other mementoes and should sell well. especially during the holidays." When my wife returned, she disagreed and voiced the opinion that they would be "slow movers". She was correct.

Three weeks later a customer said to me, "Say, you must sell a lot of those little boxes. They're all over the shop." "Actually", I replied, "I haven't sold a one but that 'silver tongued devil' that came through here three weeks ago could sure sell em!"

Another strange item acquired was a winter muff. Why would a winter muff attract attention? One reason is that young people have never seen one, except perhaps in an old family picture. They were made to match a lady's winter coat. Their primary function was to keep a lady's hands warm, however, at a cold football game, a small flask could be conveniently stored away.

We usually had an attractive sofa or settee on display at shows as a "show" or center piece and my wife used to add a pair of opera gloves and the muff as decorations. One of the most frequently asked questions was "Is it alive?" Other shoppers would say, "I'm afraid to touch it!" Youngsters at the show would observe it closely and carefully from a comfortable distance and some would advance and eventually have the courage to stroke it like a pet kitten. "I finally told my wife to remove it", I told another dealer, "No one looked at the settee but they surely liked the muff!" We still have the bloom in' thing.

One of the weirdest chairs I have ever seen belonged or did belong to a music box specialist from Pennsylvania. This man had all varieties of music boxes from the tiny Swiss-made ones, to the great disc players which ran in cost into the thousands of dollars. Also the large Swiss, German and early American table models were beautiful and expensive. They had a melodic tone not matched by other musical instruments. His collection also included player pianos and accordions. We visited him primarily to have phonographs repaired that were beset with problems beyond my basic ability to restore.

"Let me show you something very unusual", he said to me during one of our visits. I thought he was referring to a miniature "one man band", a mechanical device he had on display. "That is a dandy". I said, "If I could afford it, I'd take it right out of here." "You're looking at the 'one man band' ", he said, "I mean this chair. Sit down on it and see what happens." I did and to my surprise the chair played a tune. When I got up from the chair, it stopped playing. He told me it was European and very expensive. "Did this invention foster the idea for the 'whoopie cushion'?", I asked. He gave me a look that only a professional music box man could give a rank amateur.

39

ANTIQUE ASSOCIATIONS—A HINDRANCE OR A HELP

Another branch of the antique world is the many antique associations which band together in an effort to consolidate their expertise, provide money for advertising and promote workshops where learned dealers can lecture and answer questions. One of the products of the association we joined, was a map of a large portion of the state which pointed out the locations of the members' shops. These were distributed for the customer's use and placed in a central location of individual shops as well as the display tables at antique shows.

The annual dues for membership was quite fair and its program included several interesting meetings, however, we soon discovered that there were some negative aspects concerning membership, particularly in our case. First of all, we were located in a remote location as compared to some of the others. In the structure of the organization, there appeared to be a cluster of shops around the association headquarters which was some fifty miles from our shop. The only other dealer remotely near us was some fifteen miles away. My wife and partner thought we were sort of "out of it" as far as the rest of the organization was concerned.

I thought it was worth paying the annual dues just to have a bundle of maps sent to us. In addition to the maps there was a short description of each dealer's items of merchandise. It was a helpful brochure. To indicate our relative importance in the association, our shop number on the map was 52 out of a membership of 52. Number 51 was the dealer fifteen miles from us, whom we visited from time to time. This lady was probably one of the most knowledgeable members of the association and through our experience was to become a good friend. She was unselfish with her knowledge of the antique business and was very helpful during the early days of our learning period.

Along these lines, we questioned her about the value of the workshops sponsored by the organization at various locations in the state. They appeared to be a good thing for the beginning dealers as there were lectures, group discussions and field trips to other shops and antique shows; an effort to expose the apprentice to a wide spectrum of antique activities. Our friend advised us, "Now these antique workshops are really nice, dear." When she addressed either my wife or I, we were always called "dear". "There are some drawbacks too", she would say, "I usually get there and meet so many old friends that we get to 'drinkin and talkin' and then we either miss the lecture or I don't remember what the man had to say!"

"Another thing", she would say, "Some of those people they call on to speak don't know any more about antiques than you do." At that stage of the game, the speaker wouldn't have had to know much to know more than we did about the business. She was right in some respects. The workshops we attended were beneficial and we had a wonderful time but they were usually held on a weekend and we hesitated to close our shop or we had a show scheduled. When we did attend, we tried to follow her advice, and not to celebrate beyond the learning state. The hierarchy of the association, considering our remote circumstance, rather neglected us, or that was our impression. At any rate, during the second year of our membership, I had to call, plead, and finally "lose my cool" in order to receive a shipment of maps. One of the officers of the association finally delivered them to me at one of the shows we were both attending but by that time, half of the business year had expired. With this experience behind us, we became disenchanted with this phase of the antique world and withdrew our membership. I really don't think the association headquarters missed number 52 very much.

We had no sooner exited from this group when a local association began to take shape. The nucleous of this group would be located in our immediate area and the membership would not extend beyond the county boundaries. The neighboring county would have a familiar set-up and would exchange ideas about a brochure. It appeared to be a practical approach to a new association concept.

The local man who did most to promote the project had the viewpoint that the main effort would be advertising; the brochure and map idea again. There would be no workshops or field trips and meetings would be held when deemed necessary. The only cost would be for the brochure. The neighboring county was going to use the same procedure for its shops and we would have a reciprocal exchange of booklets. There was a good response in both counties and the association went to press.

41

Our business alone distributed thousands of the brochures at various shows over the years. There was no way to tell if these booklets had any positive effect on our sales. The only testing method would have been to ask every customer how they found the location of the shops. It would have been a difficult matter for twenty or twenty-five dealers to conscientiously conduct such a survey. "That's for a survey team to investigate", one member stated. What survey team? We genius types overlooked this factor in the organizational stage.

The only comment we heard over the years was from a dealer who told us some people from Pittsburg, PA, and had been in his shop and told him they saw the brochure at an antique show at the Shrine Mosque there. We had exhibited at this show a week prior. We eventually withdrew from this group also. We felt our best advertising was already established by a core of customers who vocally spread the word about our shop and merchandise. Our only advertising effort from then on was with the Antique Weekly Journals whose readers are sincerely interested in happenings of the antique world.

One of the humorous comments made by a local dealer was, "No more for me", he said, "people come in here, read those things, then go to someone else's shop!" My daughter commented, "Doesn't he realize people read 'those things' in other shops and visit his place?" "Who knows?", I replied, "We'll have to ask the survey team, wherever they may be."

THE ART OF BUYING

Some of the large department store chains have professional buyers who travel about our country and select merchandise. We really didn't think about this factor until our son, whom we considered a rank amateur in antique buying, pulled off the acquisition of the year. He had married a girl from one of the farming areas of a neighboring county and, of course, they visited her relatives from time to time. Next to their relatives' farm was a large tract of land upon which was located an abandoned house. My son and his wife were walking one afternoon and ventured into this old building. There they found an old cabinet, made of

Antiquarian and author Buchanan at a Washington, D.C., antique show.

My wife at the Washington, D.C., antique show.

rough lumber, falling apart and full of splinters; very primitive in nature.

My son borrowed his father-in-law's pick-up truck and moved this mass of lumber to the back of our shop where he proceeded to "clean it up". To further add to the unattractive appearance of this furniture, he painted it an ugly shade of brown. At this point he had the nerve to ask me if he could put it on the floor in our shop. We shuddered at the idea, but after all, he was our son and a fine son at that. How could we refuse? He and his wife had helped us prepare our shop for business by cleaning, painting and decorating.

We sold this "what-ever-it-was" for an excellent profit, the second day it was on the floor, to an Air Force Officer and his wife. We then decided that Robert's instincts surpassed ours. He is now stationed in Germany as the First Sergeant of an Ordnance Company. We pray for his return and some additional demonstrations of his buying talent.

To illustrate my talent as a buyer, consider the black stuffed squirrel I came upon in Virginia. It is mounted on a thick bark from a gum tree and when you hang it on a wall properly, it looks like its running up the tree! The lecture to the customer concerning this replica of animal life takes about five minutes. We have given the lecture about two hundred times. According to the taxidermists we have consulted, this particular breed of squirrel has only two habitats, North Dakota and Western Canada. The shape of the head, the length of the tail, the black fur and the dark, beady eyes are particular characteristics of this cousin of the regular squirrel. Also, their claws are longer and sharper. We tire of lecturing. The usual response from the customer is "Thank You", or "Amazing"!, after which the customer departs. This one has found the habitat of a stuffed black squirrel. Our home. Hurry home, son, and sell this creature for us.

We have many wonderful items of merchandise which we collected on buying trips. We have decided that our true motive in buying them was to preserve them for posterity. Some of the items are now decorative objects in our home and have been there for some time, as much as five years as a matter of fact.

One of our dealer friends, suggested that we establish a "Five Year Room" in our shop, consolidating all our long-range merchandise and advertising them as such. We did so and arranged them in one room. We posted a sign over the door which read, "FIVE YEAR ROOM—REDUCED PRICES". We had many visitors look at this room but no buyers. They simply enjoyed browsing in this room with all the quaint items for sale. My friend then advised us that we had a second alternative which was to place a sign on an easel at the entrance to the room reading, MUSEUM—FIVE DOLLAR ENTRANCE FEE." He assured me this would work but the plan failed. The visitors merely looked through the door at the merchandise, did not pay the entrance fee and went their merry way.

The most controversial items purchased in recent years were two oval picture frames with a sort of fancy gold trimming which were about six inches in length. Into one of these frames we inserted a picture of my wife, my daughter, Chris, and myself. The picture was taken at an amusement center on my daughter's birthday. I wore a Civil War uniform, Confederate, complete with sword; my wife and daughter wore long gowns and carried beautiful parasols. I told some of my friends that it was a picture of my great-grandfather and his family and some of them believe me. In the second frame we put a picture of my son and his wife; he wore a Union uniform with sword and she a dark gown with a very large hat. Their picture was taken at a different amusement center and they looked very neat in appearance. We always took them to antique shows as "good luck" pieces but we could have sold them fifty times. Being fairly honest, we tell the customers that they are family pictures and the frames could be obtained at any department store for about seventy five cents. We sometimes feel we should have a hundred prints made and buy a gross of frames.

Another interesting purchase, we thought, nearly became another family heirloom. It was an 1887 Remington twelve gauge shotgun which we found in Kentucky. The Remington Company was noted for the manufacture of rifles rather than shotguns. As far as we were concerned, this made it a collector's item. IT WAS. It belonged to OUR collection. We finally sold it to a customer from "guess where?", Kentucky from whence it came.

One of the most attractive of our semi-permanent fixtures was an Austrian server. It was six and one half feet in height, primarily made of Mahogany wood and had recessed mirrors on both sides of the front. There was a centered cabinet in the upper portion, a pull-out serving tray, and two very large shelves in the bottom portion, covered by two oval shaped doors. All the doors had an inlaid design resembling a spider's web. The whole inside of the piece was lined with bird's eye maple. This was an item of beautifully crafted classical furniture. We took it to several shows and displayed it in our shop for four years. We can understand why some merchandise will not sell but this item was a real mystery.

Finally, it was sold to a dealer on South Street in Philadelphia, PA. The history and movement of this item led us to call it "The Traveling Antique". We had procured it from a local dealer who had found it at a sale in Alexandria, VA. It had belonged to a lawyer there. The Philadelphia dealer sold it to a buyer from Buffalo, NY, who then sold it to a dealer from Cleveland, OH.

A lawyer from Washington, D.C. bought it in Cleveland and transported it back to his office. Later he decided to move his office and not having room for this piece of furniture, sold it to a lawyer friend from Alexandria, VA. We drove there to shop on occasion. At one time we had some legal problems with our business and consulted this lawyer who was recommended as one who had dealt with situations involving antique transactions. When we entered his office, our old Austrian server greeted us once again. After our legal discussion, the lawyer asked us our opinion of his new purchase. We told him it was an unusual piece of furniture and it had been around a long time, emphasizing, "around".

As we left I told Adaline, "Once that thing started to move, we should have equipped it with a set of wheels and a motor."

SHOPPING—THE TENNESSEE CONNECTION

Each year our Oriental Band, a unit of the Kena Temple Shrine Mosque at Fairfax, Virginia, travel to a Jamboree and compete with other bands in the Southern Association. During April, 1988, we traveled to Johnson City, Tennessee, where the event was held that year. The band charters a bus for these trips to accommodate the Shriners and their wives but we decided to drive our mini-van in order to do some shopping on the way to the

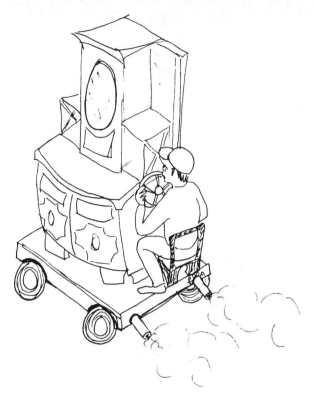

Jamboree and on our return trip home. We also planned to meet some old friends I hadn't seen for some thirty years and whom I wanted my wife to meet. All being retired school people, I knew they would get along well.

They arrived the day of the Jamboree as they lived about an hour's drive from Johnson City in the foothills of the Great Smokies. They found my wife in the crowd because Beth and Bob, my friends, looked for a lady in a green and yellow jacket who looked like a school teacher. After my band competed, we talked and discovered that they too were antique dealers. We visited Jonesboro, a village close by, had lunch and looked through a few antique shops. Prior to lunch, my wife had purchased a piece of glassware. She placed it on the floor next to her chair during lunchtime. Naturally, we forgot it when we left and never saw it again. Easy come, easy go.

Nevertheless, we were impressed with the shopping opportunities in this area and decided to return later in the summer to renew our friendship and do some serious antiquing. We returned in July with both vans just in case the hunting was good.

This was the case, as we returned home five days later, with both vans full of merchandise. Some funny things happened on the way to Tennessee. Going through North Carolina, we stopped at an antique mall for a couple of hours. My wife saw a nice walnut oval-shaped table in one of the shops, which we purchased and asked the dealer, "What do you call a table like this one?" He answered our question with "I call it a little walnut oval-shaped table." Well said. We also bought what was described as a "Plantation Desk", very unusual and primitive in nature. We later discovered that the top and bottom of this item did not exactly match and we vowed never to buy another one in a dimly lighted shop.

We stopped in Ashland, North Carolina, overnight and pressed on to Newport, Tennessee, the following day from where we called our friends for further directions. Beth answered my call and I thought it strange when she told me, "You'll have to call back, John, because there's the biggest black bear I've ever seen right out here in our yard and I can't talk to you until he goes away." "Ah, don't worry about that. I brought my rifle with me", I said because I thought she was kidding. Her voice was shaky over the phone as she shouted, "Just do as I say! This is not a joke!" We called back later; the bear had departed and we set out to find our destination. The best of directions in the "Smokies" can be misinterpreted and we toured the area a bit before I called our friends again for more instructions. This time we decided to meet at the local Post Office and follow them home.

The remainder of the day was wonderful. Bob had moved an old log cabin from another location and had it erected on his property. He was installing a kitchen, plumbing, and had restored a beautiful fireplace in the living room. A mountain stream ran through the property and the water was clear as a bell. Close by was a campground and this explained the arrival of the bear, who was looking for a free meal. We visited the rest of the day and went after Tennessee antiques the next morning with a two-pronged attack. Bob and I took the small van and my wife and Beth the large one. Beth does beautiful paintings on wood and metal, so my first purchase was an iron coffee pot for her to paint for us.

My other acquisitions of the day were four phonographs which I bought from a man in Knoxville. Bob said the man did not like to sell to dealers as he did shows as well so I paid him retail prices for them and they were well worth it. The man had a garage full of them and they were ready for the shop floor. In addition, he had one of the most comprehensive collections of phonographs and music boxes I have ever seen, which he gladly let us examine. We had one little problem with one of the phonographs. We discovered the crank was missing after we had loaded it in the van and, of course, the search was on. The search consumed another hour of shopping time but it was worth it. I told Bob, "If I can

This old sea chest from Holland was acquired from Smokie's in Tennessee in 1988.

continue to buy these, I'll never restore another one myself." This did not work out as I was never able to purchase another one from him. I hope my check for the others did not bounce because I don't want to return to Tennessee and find my picture on the Post Office bulletin board. Later in the day I bought five sets of white porcelain door knobs, now a rarity. If anyone wants a set, let me know.

My wife filled the large van with merchandise but saved a little space for the walnut, oval-shaped table we bought in North Carolina to pick up on the return trip to our home. The best item she found was an old sea chest, so old the metal bands, which were hand forged, were beginning to deteriorate. It measured six feet, by two and a half feet, by three and half feet and must have weighed one hundred and fifty pounds. We were told by the seller that a Community College instructor in Newport, Tennessee, had researched the item with the following history resulting: It had originated in the Netherlands during the 1700's and was used for a family to cross the ocean. The family then settled in Pennsylvania. In 1833 it was painted blue with red roses in a center wreath arrangement. It was found in a mountain hamlet by the name of Bully Gap, Tennessee, which is noted in the *Rand and McNally Road Atlas*.

The owners who sold it said, "It's too old and no good." It belongs in a museum but we haven't found a museum willing to buy it, as yet.

One of my friends advises me, "John, if you never sell it, don't worry about it. It will fit you perfectly." Not funny.

SHOPPING—THE PENNSYLVANIA CONNECTION

In the early days after our entry into the antique world, my son and I decided to take a short vacation together and while we were doing so, do some antique buying. We chose Pennsylvania, because I had seen some items there previously, that I wanted to look at again.

We had met a dealer at one of the Maryland shows who hailed from a small village just North of the Pennsylvania border. He had shown us a picture of a lady's desk that attracted us and he wanted to sell it. This was our first stop, where we bought the desk. The dealer was not there so we conducted our business with the lady of the house who resembled the dealer to a marked degree. On departing, I told her, "I saw a picture of this desk your brother and his wife had at a Maryland show." There was no comment except she thanked me and we went our way.

We drove on and came across a fascinating shop in the tourist area where PENNSYLVANIA DUTCH cooking prevails. There was a barn-sized building containing tons of antiques of all sorts and sizes. Being a large building, there were larger items than you would ordinarily find in a typical shop. There was a pump from an old gasoline station; a type with the large glass container on top so you could actually see the gallons diminish as the automobile was filled. There were two old cars, one a "Model T" Ford and an old hearse, the style and vintage debatable. Next came an array of old stop signals, both railway and highway. The items of old clothing and uniforms were numerous and there was an amazing collection of old tools. My big mistake here was not buying a barrel full of wooden shafted golf clubs which had a low price for the lot. Being a rank amateur at the time, I thought it would be too much work to clean them up. Later I learned that the real golf club collectors don't want them cleaned. A friend of mine had a set of these clubs refinished and sent the heads to a golf club manufacturer to be rechromed. They were beautiful, but their authenticity had been destroyed. "Well, my friend told me, "they'll look nice mounted on the wall of my den."

My son and I had the same problem with buying at that stage of the game. We did not have the ability to see many items in their proper state of repair or placed in the proper setting. My son remarked, "We should have brought Mom along. She'd know what she was doing." I thanked him for his vote of confidence and we continued our travels.

At another shop a few more miles down the road we found some interesting items in a half-hardware store and half-antique shop. We saw an interesting pitcher and bowl set, lavishly hand painted and I did have enough experience with these items to know it was very old. We also saw a legitimate set of cigar molds. My wife and I had purchased a set previously and used them for wall decorations in one of our rooms at home which had been panelled with dark wood. The proprietor told us, "There's a lot more of them in the basement." My son went down to the basement and returned with another set. He told the proprietor, "There's a lot of them down there but look Dad, they're new." The proprietor remarked, "That's right, they are new but in a hundred years they'll be antiques. Ha! Ha! Ha!" We bought a small child's rocking chair and moved on.

Next we moved into an area of the farm country where a lot of smoked meat is prepared. One company had an outlet store and we bought Lebanon bologna, thick sliced smoked bacon and smoked pork chops as the Germans call it, "Ripschen". We dined at a restaurant which served Pennsylvania Dutch, "all you can eat" type dinners, "stoking ourselves up" for the next day's traveling. As for this day, we felt we had done quite well with our buying.

The next day we reversed our direction to the West and entered an area which you could safely designate as an antique oriented complex of shops and warehouses. Between two large cities, approximately forty miles apart, we estimated there were thirty-five shops. One little town had at least six shops and in addition, a fine German restaurant where we "stoked up" again at lunchtime.

On this segment of the trip we picked up some more items. One, the dealer told us, was called "end-of-day glass". The glass makers, at the end of the day, poured all their left over molten glass into a common mold, whatever the colors might be. The result was unpredictable but I thought this particular piece was beautiful. I admired it for its uniqueness and was rather regretful when it eventually sold. We also found a phonograph with a broken spring. My son asked, "Don't you ever buy one that works?" I told him to find a mint condition phonograph and if I could afford it, I'd buy it.

Later, after searching through what seemed like an endless chain of shops, I bought eight beautiful cranberry glasses for my wife's birthday. We also saw a nice Victorian sofa with beautiful carving and in addition, had its original horsehair upholstery. My wife and I returned and bought this excellent sofa at a later date.

To conclude the day, we visited the Gettysburg battlefield.

Since I was retired from the Army and my son was on active duty, we enjoyed the self-guided tour of the area.

Upon our return home, thinking we had made a worthwhile effort with our buying, my wife evaluated our purchases. She thought the "end-of-day-glass" was ugly, the rocking chair leaned back too far and the phonograph needed too much work. She liked her birthday gift, the cranberry glasses, but she said, "I hate to tell you this, as your heart was in the right place, but they're new ones." Also, the pitcher from the pitcher and bowl set was chipped. "You think we ought to go back and start over?", my son asked. "No", I replied, "after she has some Lebanon bologna, bacon and smoked pork she'll be less critical."

At a later date. I met the dealer from whom I had purchased the small desk. "You got me in trouble when you stopped by for the desk", he said. "You told my wife you saw a picture of it her brother and his wife showed you." "She looked so much like you, I thought it was your sister", I replied. "No that was my wife but that *wasn't* my wife at the show!" Accidents do happen in strange places.

SHOPPING—THE OHIO—WEST VIRGINIA CONNECTION

Sometime during each summer we like to return to our home town to visit friends and some of our former teachers. My wife "antiques" and I try to play some golf. The best visits are during our high school reunions when more than the usual number of old friends are present and everyone is in a good frame of mind. Since my wife and I grew up together, we attend her reunions and mine whenever they occur. I always thought my graduating class had a fine reputation until a couple of years ago when one of our former teachers, whom we all admired, referred to my class as "Johnny's Gang". Perhaps we were not seeing ourselves through the eyes of others.

I made a short trip a few years back to visit my cousins in Ohio and West Virginia and play golf with some of my old classmates at home. One of them told me he had a fine dining room set he wanted to sell as he and his wife were moving from a large home to a small townhouse. The set had been given to him by an aunt and considering the years involved, it would have to be classified as antique. The set consisted of a beautiful round light cherry table, four chairs, a server and a china closet. It had been refinished once by a man who had been our manual arts teacher when we attended high school. He had done a professional job of refinishing, naturally, and this added some special significance to the purchase on our part.

I asked my friend to save it for me until I returned home and discussed buying it with my wife. I regretted not having my polaroid camera with me at the time but I was able, upon returning home, to convince my wife I had found a prize antique dining room outfit. We took our large van and returned to Ohio the next day.

By this time I began to feel like I had spent a good portion of my life behind the wheel of that van. That afternoon we finished the purchasing transaction, packed the set well, visited awhile and then the "roadrunners" were off again. We crossed the Ohio river and had safely passed through about half of West Virginia when we saw an ANTIQUE sign pointing towards a small village. After turning off the main highway, we wound around hills and vales, as well as up and down hills and vales; mostly up! When the houses and barns below the road appeared to be about an inch long, I wondered if we would ever arrive at the mountain village. My wife is afraid of height and I could tell when she was getting "edgy" when she asked, "Did you pack the parachutes?"

We finally overcame the challenge of this road and arrived safely at the village. We located the shop and there were a number of interesting items including a monstrosity my wife bought called a leather-stretcher. This thing was about six feet long, made with old lumber, now deteriorating somewhat and had a seat, apparently for the operator, whatever he did with the thing. The proprietor of the shop told me a man sat on the seat and pulled a lever which stretched the leather which was fastened to the other end. I was fascinated with this contraption but never could really see the usefulness of this jumble of wasted lumber. I TOLD Adaline, "I think I'll write a story entitled, 'I RISKED OUR LIVES ON A WEST VIRGINIA MOUNTAIN FOR A LEATHER-STRETCHER'."

This marvelous acquisition in hand, we pressed on and eventually arrived back at the main highway. We put some more miles behind us and as we approached the Maryland border my wife saw a sign which read "YARD SALE". I looked and it not only read "YARD SALE" but "HUGE YARD SALE". Of course we couldn't resist this type of temptation and exited from the main highway once more. It wasn't long before we realized we had imposed another driving challenge on ourselves. After many "ups, downs and around", the hard surfaced road turned to a gravel surface. We were about to turn back when we saw the second "HUGE YARD SALE" sign. The arrow actually pointed up so up we went, for miles. My wife was doing the driving at the time and remarked, "I always luck out and get the good roads when it's my turn to drive." I commented, "We are strange people. We drive four hundred miles to pick up a fine set of furniture and then bounce it around on a dirty, dusty mountain road!"

Miraculously, we arrived on a plateau where there was, in fact, a huge yard sale in progress. We looked about the sale, had a good lunch and continued browsing. I spotted a book of Kipling's stories in a large box of books and inquired about it. The man selling the books said I could have the whole box for five dollars but since I was "book poor" at the time, I thanked him and started to walk away. Then he asked, "Do you like to read?" I answered in the affirmative and he said, "Go ahead and take it free, enjoy it and come back and see us." I didn't take his name but will always remember his generosity. I told him I would return sometime if I ever had the courage to negotiate the mountain road again.

We were getting closer and closer to the Maryland border when curiosity overcame us again and we left the main highway to visit an antique shop just off to the right; no mountain road to stand in our way this time. The shop was situated near a large motel and we suspected inflated prices but were surprised that their merchandise was very reasonably tagged. I fell for a large Shirley Temple picture that had been used on a theatre marquee years ago. Such a picture this size was a rarity in our area and I did sell it for a good price when we returned to our shop.

The dealer showed my wife three items that he swore would bring a big price in Maryland. They were old lightning rods with the glass insulators attached. There was a single upright leg supported by three legs in a tripod arrangement with the glass fixture in the middle. I thought it was one of the ugliest things I had ever seen. My wife bought them! I said, "I think you have lost all your perspective, Dear. First a leather-stretcher and now these silly things!" "I know what I'm doing", was her reply. She was right. She sold them immediately upon our return to the shop. "Bite your tongue, John", was my thought.

Once back in our home state, we visited an old friend and fellow dealer in a small Maryland-Pennsylvania border town. He had an interesting shop and always offered us a "cold one" when we stopped to visit. He told us about a local bakery which he highly recommended. We said our "goodbye's" and visited the bakery where we bought a pie and two loaves of raisin bread. This raisin bread was the best I had ever eaten and my family agreed with me. A few days later my wife said, "Well, that was a nice fast trip. What did you like most about it?" "The raisin bread, of course", I said, "every time I have a piece of it I can tolerate the leather-stretcher and the lightning rods a little better."

HERE THEY COME—TWO BY TWO'S
(OR THREE'S)

"Here they come, two by two", are words from a popular 1940's song rendered by the Mills Brothers. "Sweethearts on parade", the words roll on. When they come to the antique shop or show, they may be sweethearts but rarely do they agree or like the same things. Don't misunderstand my feelings, but the greater percentage of mixed shopping ends up on the negative side. The mixture really doesn't make much difference. There may be two women, two men, three women or three men. Mother and daughter may be together, father and son, father and mother with son or daughter, boy with girlfriend, relatives, friends, or many other combinations. When a single shopper approaches, man or woman, we feel we have a fighting chance of making a sale. When multiple shoppers appear we then prepare for two or three answers to questions, rather than just one. In addition, more time is consumed on questions and explanations when the combination shoppers appear, and for the most part, no sales result. More factors

This is Claudia, our mannequin. We've used her at many shows. She's wearing an 1890 gown.

enter the equation when more than one person is involved. During a local show, Adaline was showing a beautiful still life painting, representing a hunter's collection of weapons and trophies.

The gun, the powder horn, a rabbit and a squirrel mounted, a forest hat, wild flowers and other forest greenery, all over a beautiful mantel and fireplace. The frame was rustic and lent to the forest scene. It was conducive to a man's den or library. The shopper, a lady, told my wife, "I'm going to find my husband to see if he likes it. If he does, I'm going to buy it for his birthday and up to now, I had no idea what to give him." When she found him and returned to the booth, he appraised the picture, frowned and said something about being tired of looking at antiques and further more, it was time for them to leave and go to a "crab feast" they were to attend on that day. He stomped off but his wife continued to admire the picture. Two other couples also came by and reminded her it was time to go to the "crab feast and Bill, her husband, had already left the show. The wife said, "Yes, and the biggest crab is out in the car!" She further stated, "I'm so mad at him now, I'll be back and buy it anyway, whether he likes it or not. I like it!" In this instance a disagreement worked in our favor but such is not generally the case.

At another show, a young lady entered the booth and admired a wicker baby carriage, we had displayed. The girl remarked that it would go with some other wicker she decorated her flower shop with on occasion. She then departed with the statement, "I'm going to find my mother and get her opinion." My nerves immediately began to act up. Mother and daughter returned, examined the carriage and the fight was on. "You need a baby carriage like you need three eyes. You aren't pregnant, are you?, she shouted. The daughter shouted back, "What a lousy thing to say! If I was pregnant, you'd be the first to know about it, nosey!" Then the mother said the price was too high and they departed, still fighting. They came fighting and left fighting. No sale. There were other people in the booth and they gave a sigh of relief when they left, that you could have heard three booths away.

A major case of conflict took place at a very large show where over two hundred dealers were exhibiting. We had acquired a Civil War vintage wedding gown and my wife had purchased a mannequin in order to display it. It was a beautiful gown with a bodice, hoops and all for the bustle, etc. It looked great on the mannequin and attracted a lot of attention. A young lady told my wife she loved the gown. "I'm going to a costume ball soon and this would be ideal. I wonder if it would fit me?", she asked. My wife told her she could try it on if she liked. The business of trying on the gown turned into an unrehearsed comedy. The young lady had worn blue jeans and a short sleeved shirt, thus she put the gown on over these. The hilarious part came about in getting the dress off the mannequin as the arms had to be removed and the body separated at the waist. Throughout this procedure an interested crowd gathered; some even took pictures of the girl in the dress. It fitted perfectly. A sale! The crowd increased in size which delighted us no end. Meanwhile, the mannequin stood there in front of the crowd, naked. While inanimate, she was very shapely and had beautiful lifelike eyes. A neighboring dealer discreetly covered her with a quilt she had for sale. The crowd loved it!

Now the unhappy part occurred. Now came the husband onto the scene and was apparently upset about the attention his wife was receiving from the crowd. "What are you doing with that silly dress on?", he asked. "I'm going to buy it for the ball", she answered matter-of-factly. "No way!", he retorted, "take it off and let's go home. I'm hungry." They left in a cloud of exclamations directed at each other, none complimentary. No sale. Ah, for the single customer.

I won't go into the confusion that occurs when three or more shoppers get together. They measure, they speculate, they argue and even get jealous of the ones who may want and could afford the item in question. They also give the history of a relative who had a similar item at one time. I shouldn't criticize too much as some of these conversations are quite humorous.

One customer liked one of our Victor phonographs and really wanted to buy it. She told her shopping mate, a girlfriend, "I just got a bonus on my job and I'd like to have that but my husband doesn't like music." The girlfriend replied, "It's your money. If you like it, you ought to buy it." She told us she didn't know what to do and actually came back to the shop three times to admire it, listen to it, but still could not make a decision. I began to wonder if she were afraid of her husband's reaction and she ventured to say this was the case. I told her, "Then you better not buy it. I hate to miss a sale but I would also hate to deliver it. A sale is not worth a black eye."

THE TWO BY TWO'S (OR THREE BY THREE'S)—IN SYNC

We told of some of the problems associated with multiple shoppers but stated that on occasion people do shop in harmony and watching and dealing with them is a joy. Most of the syncopated customers are husband and wife or young couples, engaged to be married, who are looking for merchandise to furnish a new apartment or home. Their general wants are furniture, rugs, lamps, pictures, etc., and we have sold a goodly number of old phonographs, records and music boxes. The young people are especially fascinated with old music players and records. They know what they are looking for and when they find it, they are willing to buy, if the price is right or a suitable arrangement can be made for payment plans or lay-away agreements.

One of the first such sales was at a local High School show sponsored by The Lions Club. I had found a Victor phonograph that played well but was an eyesore in appearance. Having been a paper pusher all my life, I was surprised that I could do a decent job of refinishing. I also shined up the metal parts and cleaned the motor. This was my first effort at restoring a phonograph and it took some time, but I enjoyed it because I like music. The first day of the show, a young couple looked and listened to my refurbished machine. The young man told his wife, "I've always wanted one of these but was never able to find one in this state of repair. It looks as good as it did in 1916."

One funny thing about the restoration was that the knob was missing on the end of the crank. My personal vehicle at the time was a Pacer. This car will someday be a collector's item as it is no longer manufactured by AMC; maybe I should have saved it for future value. I took the knob off the end of the gear shift and put it on the phonograph. It worked beautifully. Adaline said, "That looks like the knob off the gear shift of the Pacer." "It is", I said, "but I'll get another one at the auto store." I never found another as AMC quit making the spare parts for this model. The couple agreed on the purchase and we still see them at other shows. The phonograph is still playing beautifully and they are still listening cheerfully. God bless them. The husband is a piano player and entertains in fine restaurants and he is partial to "big

band" music. We gave him a pack of needles and ten records to start his collection.

An act of generosity sometimes leads to a sale you hadn't counted on. A young man, his wife and son, probably a fourth grader, looked through our shop. We had an Edison phonograph, one of the large floor models, on display. The Edison has a very true recording tone and a better volume control than most of the "old timers". "Could we hear it play?", the father asked. I responded by playing a record and explaining to them some of the unique features of the Edison such as the automatic stop, the moving horn, the volume control and the double spring which allows it to play more records than others, before having to wind it again. "The boy is working on a school report on Edison", the mother informed me, "and that demonstration will help. How much is one of those thick records?", she asked. I had a large collection at the time and they were selling quite well. I told the mother, "Since he is one of the youngsters doing his home work now-a-days, I'll donate the record." I was surprised how much the little fellow appreciated it.

About six months later a huge RV pulled up in the front of our shop and out of it came the same family. After greetings, the father said, "Allen wants to thank you again for the record you gave him. It helped him with his school report and he hasn't forgotten about it. They bought the Edison that day and we loaded it into the RV. They were traveling from Vermont on their way to Florida. We laughed as they pulled away, a long drive ahead of them but the only tourists in captivity with an Edison phonograph aboard. They drove away happily, the Edison playing merrily. God Bless!

We decided during August, 1989, to give up the management of the antique complex and close our shop over the winter months. After a show in Pittsburg, PA, we unloaded our fine merchandise at home, which turned out to be a blessing in disguise. A week later, a neighboring dealer suffered a fire which destroyed most of her merchandise. We had only smoke damage and as we cleaned it we moved it home into spare bedrooms and storage sheds, our children having long since departed. We did save one room at home for occasional guests. Two weeks later an even worse fire occurred and this time our shop and two others were gutted. The center was condemned by the fire marshall until it could be properly restored.

One gentleman had purchased, at a considerably high price, a seven foot mantel with a large mirror. It was golden oak and had been restored to perfection. It was the only large item left in the shop at the time of the fire. Arriving at the center on the morning of the fire, the fireman were about to hose down the shop for the second time and asked me what they should do with the mantel. I told them to throw it on the lawn in front of the shop. My feeling was that it was a total loss and my intention was to forget about it. My wife had the foresight not to give up on it and some friends put it in their barn nearby until we could work on it. Our furniture expert said he thought we could salvage it by airing it out, getting the smell of smoke out of it and cleaning it.

I called the customer who had bought the mantel to tell him I thought the fire had ruined it and I would be sending his money back to him. "Please don't be so pessimistic", he said, "give it a try. My sweetheart made four stained glass fixtures for the corners of the mirror and she'll be brokenhearted if I don't bring the mantel home." Much time was taken in airing the mantel out and cleaning it, *but it was delivered!*

One of our friends said, "I read about a man in India who loved his wife so much he built the Taj Mahal for her. This customer of yours didn't do anything that great but he must have had the same kind of affection for his wife." We feel the same. God Bless!

PETE—THE WATCHCAT

Crime being at a high level now-a-days, the police advise we have a lot of lights in and about our homes and businesses. They also suggest a good watchdog, particularly one that barks loudly, like mine. He's a watchdog but he wakes me more often with his loud barking than he scares off intruders in the night. We have pondered about this problem at our shop but it is very difficult to keep a dog in a shop. By accident, we stumbled across the answer to our predicament.

One Sunday afternoon a cat, yellow with white stripes, wandered into our shop; a tomcat by the way. He was nice and clean

and wore a flea collar, so I assumed he had an owner. After awhile he scratched at the door and we let him out. Later I watched him walking up and down the street in front of the other shops. Occasionally he would enter a shop and sooner or later exit, once by benefit of a broom swiping near his tail-end. Later in the evening he was still wandering around and so I thought his owner's hadn't left the area. At closing time, he was still around and so I asked some of the shopkeepers if he belonged to one of them. One dealer told me he thought he saw the cat get out of a car from Virginia; all the Virginia cars were gone. We later decided he had been "dumped" by people tired of their pet. Although most people would disapprove of this tactic, it does happen sometimes.

My wife advised me, "If he's still around tomorrow we better feed him." This turned out to be the case. I brought some food from home and the cat followed me into the shop and ate. As you can surmise, he was now OUR cat.

The following day he was still there, of course, ready to eat. That night I left him in the shop as my wife had fixed a box for him to sleep in. Eventually he became attached to me and began sitting on my lap. I had an easy chair in the shop and a small portable TV. I spent more time at the shop, at that time, than my wife and on slow days or weekends the cat and I would watch baseball or football.

Some nights he would stay out until morning and others he would spend in the shop. One night the complex manager looked into one of our windows and the cat scratched at him and hissed, showing his sharp, glistening teeth. Having recovered from the shock, the manager called me and asked, "Do you know there's a cat in your shop?" "Yes", I replied, "someone dropped him off about a week ago and I'm waiting for them to come back and pick him up. We have made several calls to the surrounding radio stations but there had been no response, as yet." "Well", he continued, "he went mad when I looked in the window. He's really tearing that place apart!" I thought I had better return to the shop and see what damage was done but when I arrived the cat greeted me as usual, and I noticed he had not broken a thing. He broke nothing in the year and a half with us. But he was a fine "watchcat". He would raise some fuss if anyone looked in the window or tried a door.

He also kept our shop free of mice, rats and other critters, but his real culinary preference was the tiny ground squirrels; they were in abundance on the lawn and other land surrounding the complex. There were some snakes around as well. The dealer next to me, whose name was Peter, told me one day, "If you'd feed that cat once in awhile, he wouldn't hunt so much." "It's his nature to hunt", I answered. "It's also his nature", he continued, "to bring those ground squirrels right up in front of us, when we're sitting outside, and eat them. Does he have to eat them in front of somebody in order to enjoy them?" I told him I would talk to the cat about the problem. "By the way", I said, "We have decided to call the cat Pete, after you", (I inwardly grinned). "When I call him don't you come running, also." He didn't smile at me.

Pete was the gentlest cat around; that is, during the daytime when he ate, slept and was admired and petted by hundreds of children. He also, during the day, consumed great amounts of "goodies" offered him by his little friends. This prepared him for the night when he turned into a type of werewolf. In the mornings when I would arrive at the shop, he would be laying by the door exhausted, dirty, hungry, sleepy and several times beat senseless, bloody and torn. He had one bloody red eye and one clear green one left. Peter, the neighboring dealer, advised, "If you want to keep that cat in one piece you had better get his 'fixed'." Thus we took the inevitable trip to the Veterinarian and we learned just how expensive and valuable this animal was to us.

This accomplished, Pete traveled less and never, to the best of my knowledge, fought again. There wasn't anything left to fight about now and he was tranquil, day and night. He tended to sleep more but when anyone looked in a window, he turned into a youthful tiger.

I saw a small snake wiggle under some molding one day and Pete saw it as well. The next day, there lay the snake, dead. Pete sat there, looking on proudly.

In winter, when he would not be back by the time we closed the shop, he would call on our resident security man. He had a small apartment in the complex and looked after things when we were all gone. During the winter, he housed the cat as much as we did but he didn't mind. Everyone loved Pete.

Our "watchcat" used to visit all the shops from time to time and never bothered any of the merchandise. One of the other

dealers bought a Labrador retriever pup and kept it in the shop with him during the day. Ole Pete wandered in one day, not having been introduced to the new resident, and the Labrador, being a very gentle dog, attempted to "play" with Pete. Pete did not consider this play and made it back to our shop in seconds; he actually climbed up the screen door, trying to get back in. He and the Labrador later became friends.

One day Pete didn't return from a run; this ran into days and then weeks so we could only surmise what had happened to him. He used to play with my pencils when I worked at the desk. As I attempted bookwork, he would roll them back and forth. I miss him during the football season. One of the other dealers told me had had seen a yellow and white spot on the highway in front of the shop. I guess it was Pete, the unfortunate victim of a sixteen wheeler.

Well, we didn't have our "watchcat" very long but considering a year of human life is equal to seven for a cat, Pete was well fed, had a lot of friends and a great night life there for awhile. I know some cats who didn't do half as well.

THE PAUSE THAT REFRESHES AND EDUCATES

One very hot and humid afternoon I adjourned from our steamy shop and repaired to a nearby tavern which was airconditioned, of course. When I say it was hot and humid it is an understatement about the Potomac basin during July and August. This was before our complex was air-conditioned and the period between two and six o'clock was a stuffy, sweaty ordeal, if you could not escape from it. The week previous, we had participated in a local show in a High School where the air-conditioning system had malfunctioned. Usually, this was a very successful show, well managed and well attended but when the air-conditioning faltered everyone suffered. The customers stayed as long as they could, which was about thirty minutes at most and then departed for cooler places. As a result, the show was doomed. With this in memory and sweat pouring off my body, I hastened to the tavern for a "cool one" and a little relaxation.

The refreshing air of the tavern picked me up and my first thought was how great it would be at home today, nice and cool and a good baseball game going on television. There were nine customers at the bar as I entered and found an empty seat between two other men. The second man to my right had apparently been there longer that the others because he was talking louder and faster than the rest of them. He looked down the bar at me as I ordered a "cool one" and said, "Hey, ain't you the guy who runs the antique center down the road?" I answered that I was, indeed, that person. He looked at me through glassy eyes and asked. "You know what I think about antiques?" I replied that I had no idea what he thought, not being acquainted with him. Then I remembered he had been in our shop a couple of times. I didn't remember the face but did recall the voice. Both times he had people with him and he was doing all the talking, just as he was now.

He continued, "I think a lot of antiques are fakes. What do you think?" I answered, "I don't think there are any fake antiques but there are a lot of reproductions of antiques and sometimes it's hard to tell which is which." There was a bar customer sitting between us and I could tell by the expression of his face that he had not come to the tavern to be educated about antiques, or anything else, for that matter.

"You know what I saw?", was his next question. I told him I had not even a slight idea of what he had seen. He then informed me that he had seen reproductions of antique clocks in my shop and that he thought this was funny, since I was supposed to know reproductions when I saw them. I informed him that my shop sign read, ANTIQUES AND COLLECTIBLES, that they were NEW CLOCKS and not reproductions and that some people preferred them. This was because they did not want to pay the high price for an antique clock and the high cost of repairing them. Thus my clocks were new collectible items. He chuckled and muttered something indistinguishable.

He rambled on with, "You know, my aunt had an antique china closet and some guy offered her two hundred dollars for it and you know what I told her?" I told him I knew not what he had told her. "Well, I said", he fumbled on, "I wouldn't take less that two hundred fifty for it. What do you think?" I told him I couldn't think about it because I hadn't seen it. A mistake on my part.

With that he told me how high it was, how wide it was, how many shelves it had, where and how long it had sat in the house and other details. To end this quiz I told him she should not sell if for less than a thousand dollars. The man next to me departed, closely followed by two more customers, probably going to another place to rest their ears. The windbag moved over next to me. The tavern owner was beginning to look distressed because he was losing customers and it was early afternoon.

The verbose one offered me another "cool one". I felt I could accept it as a reward for my patience with him and the valuable information about antiques he was receiving from me. "You know what?" he asked. I said I didn't know the man. He thought this was hilarious. The remaining patrons of the tavern did not even smile. "I'll tell you what", he continued, "I know a woman who has an old settee and chair she wants to get rid of. Now I've seen em myself and I'll bet with repair and some new covers you could buy it and make a big sale?" "And wood damage?" I asked. He told me a couple of legs were off the settee and an arm off the chair along with some springs missing. I made a quick estimate of a couple of hundred dollars in repair bills. Two more bar patrons went elsewhere.

"You know what I told my sister?", he queried on. I asked him how I could possibly know and he allowed that it was sort of a silly question. He then remarked, "I told her she should sell her depression glass now, while it was "hot". I asked him if it was "hot" because it was selling well or whether she had stolen it. He was puzzled why I would think his sister would steal anything, including depression glass. "How can you tell if depression glass is real?", was his next question. I asked him the color of the glass. He said she had all colors; white, green, red, blue, pink and yellow. I informed him her best bet was to look for a book on depression glass in the library. At that time, the remaining bar patron left us.

"I know where you can pick up an old record player too, and you know who has it?", he asked. I told him I didn't know who had the record player. He told me his Grandmother had it and hadn't used it for years. We had finally gotten to Grandma and he had finally gotten to me and I left the tavern. Another customer entered as I was leaving and I thought, he can bend this guy's ear for awhile.

When I returned to the hot shop, my wife asked, "Did you get cooled off?" I informed her I certainly had and a fellow had given me some valuable information about antiques and had bought me a "cool one" to boot.

MORE SHOW NEWS—NEVER PUBLISHED

Just when we've seen all the funny things that can happen at the show or shop, a new incident pops up on the horizon. At one big show we had to go through three check points to get into the building and set up our booth. The first check was made as we arrived at the outside parking area. There they checked our name and pointed out the door we were to approach. At the next check point our names were checked again by another agent of the promoter and we were directed where to park our vehicles. A final processing was completed at the show office where we received our entry badges and paid the final balance of our booth rent. This sounds complicated but actually was very efficient. At some shows its sort of "Go! Sheepy! Go!" The amusing incident at this particular show was the entry badge incident.

We were within driving distance of home. After arranging our booth, we were able to leave and return in the morning for the first day of the exhibition. We entered the building without incident and went about our business for several hours. Around mid-afternoon one of the other dealers asked my wife, "Say, where

My wife searches for collectibles at a park show in New
Castle, Delaware, in 1989.

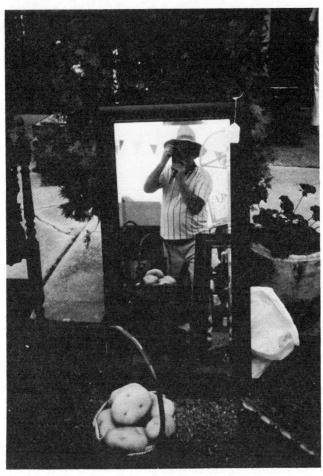

I'm taking my own picture at a street show in
North Beach, Maryland, in 1990.

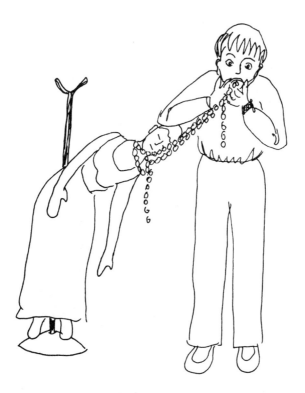

did you get that entry badge?" It read, ADALINE BUCHANAN, S.A.S.O.B.A. (Southern Atlantic Oriental Band Association, Jamboree, 1989, Fayetteville, N.C.). This was a Shrine event we attended a couple of weeks prior to this show. She had picked it up by mistake in the morning and the security man at the show entrance apparently just looked at the color, which was the same as the show badge. So much for tight security.

One of my favorite pastimes has been restoring old phonographs and displaying them at antique shows. I have found that refinishing them and repairing the mechanical parts of these machines to be interesting and profitable. We have dealt mostly with Edisons, Victrolas, Columbias and Aeoleans. At one time, when they were so popular, there were over two hundred and fifty licensed manufactures of these items in the United States alone. I was able to take care of most of the repairs on these machines except repairing or replacing springs. I send these to the professionals as some of the amateurs who have tinkered with broken springs have met with unfortunate results. A spring that has been encased in a canister for sixty or seventy years, if not handled with care and the proper tools, comes out of there like the spring of a fifty calibre machine gun. This could provide one with a twin for their navel.

These machines provided the center of attraction at many of the shows we have done and were particularly fascinating to young people who had not been exposed to them, A good phonograph and some 78 RMP (revolutions per minute), "Big Band" records attract a crowd. At one of our shows, I noticed a young couple admiring one of our machines and I approached them. "Like to hear it?", I asked. They indicated that they would and I looked for a good demonstration record. The record I selected was rather dusty and being in a hurry I used mother nature's cleaning fluid, expectorate and a handkerchief. I didn't think they witnessed this procedure as I had turned my back to them. They asked several questions and I conducted a short lecture on this model of player. They were pleased with it and bought it. I threw in some needles and records to start their collection and made arrangements for delivery the following day. To review my instructions the young man said, "Now let me see if I've got this all down. We use nice clean records, change the needle frequently, never wind it too tightly or while it is playing and to clean the records, you spit on them." They had seen my non-professional cleaning method after all, and I advised them that there were better ways of doing this.

One of the most fantastic incidents in our show experience took place at the same show. My wife had an old German-made short formal she had purchased in Weisbaden some years ago and we dressed our mannequin, Claudia as we called her, in it for this show. People admired Claudia almost as much as our phonographs. My wife had acquired a cheap set of faux pearls along the way and Claudia had these on with the formal. We were standing to one side of the booth when my wife remarked, "Look over there! That woman is biting those fake pearls!" Apparently this is an accepted method of testing the validity of real pearls and our string, being of the costume jewelry variety, did not qualify. To the lady's astonishment, she managed to get one pearl lodged onto one of her teeth and was having considerable difficulty extracting it. We decided to act as though we didn't see what was happening as she struggled with this problem.

My wife had folded the pearls several times around the mannequin's neck and thus they could not be lifted off over her head. As we watched out of the corner of our eyes, the lady searched for the clasp, found it, but it would not open for her. In final desperation, she muttered something and my wife walked across the booth to assist her. My wife couldn't get the clasp open either and called for me. By that time the lady, the mannequin, my wife and I and several curious observers were drawing a crowd.

"Can't you pull the pearl off the tooth?", my wife asked. The lady muttered something indistinguishable. It's difficult to speak properly with a string of pearls hanging out of your mouth. The woman's face was turning from pink to purple by now as the watching audience grew in size. I tried the clasp myself but the lady, having pulled and tugged at the string, had damaged the clasp and it would not budge. "Just get me the scissors and I'll cut the string", I said, "we can't keep the lady standing here all day!" This having been accomplished, the lady was free from the mannequin but there she stood in the middle of a fascinated crowd of people with a mouth full of fake pearls. We finally summoned the promoter, who arranged for a dental appointment. A man in the audience asked, "How did she get in that fix?" My wife answered, "She was trying to see if the pearls were real but it doesn't work on costume jewelry, believe me!" I know I'm not going to try it.

THE AUCTION—A MYSTERY TO THE UNTUTORED

My wife has a passion for auction sales and I have grown to like them myself if the weather, time of day, and the refreshments available are to my liking. Adaline's fondness of this facet of the antique world stems from the fact that her father took her with him to auctions when she could hardly toddle along. Her father had a kind of "checkered" approach to business, dabbling in real estate, rental properties, horse trading, horse racing, a movie theatre and old furniture. His office sign read, *WE BUY, SELL, RENT AND TRADE ANYTHING.* HE was a very practical man, although this did not appear to be the case, due to his wide range of business activities. He was in his sixties when my wife was a little girl, however, she accompanied him to many places in the adult world.

Some of her early auction experiences were very unusual. We grew up in a small town and the auctions which she attended during these formative years were usually held in even smaller villages and farms located around the county. These auctions offered items of all sorts from food, land, furniture and glass to animals. Her father taught her the finer points of "bidding", which she tried to pass on to me later in life and in this effort she failed for some time until I finally "caught on".

At one particular auction sale, a cow was offered for sale and her father, being true to his philosophy of buying and selling anything, acquired the cow for a fair price. My wife tells me they hadn't thought about one problem connected with the buying of the cow; they had no place to keep a cow! Her father somehow talked a local farmer into taking care of her for half the milk. Her mother "Nixed" any idea of using the back yard for "Cherry's" (the cow's name) new home.

Another early experience with auctions led her to begin taking piano lessons. Someone was trying to rid themselves of a perfectly good instrument which was in good shape structurally and in addition, it was in tune. You won't believe this, but no one bid on the thing and my wife bid it in for twenty-five cents! Of course, this was in the forties and the quarter still had some purchasing power.

She continued to go to auctions throughout her youthful years and early adult life. When we were married we furnished our first home in Kentucky with furniture and household items, including rugs, which she had acquired through the years at sales. In spite of her guidance it was a long time before I came close to her talent for seeing a good thing in a maze of merchandise. She always told me, "John, you have an amazing gift for paying fifty dollars for a twenty five cent item. The idea is to pay twenty five cents for a fifty dollar item." "Great! If I could only do that", was my only reply.

As all "antiquers" know, to be successful at auctions you must be able to understand and follow what the auctioneer is saying. To me, during the early stages of this learning experience, the auctioneer spoke in an incomprehensible foreign language. I had never heard an auctioneer except on old radio shows and the only phrase I understood was "Sold! American!" After the language riddle unraveled a bit for me, I was faced with learning how to bid. Being taught that the slightest movement on my part might trigger a response from the auctioneer, I conducted myself cautiously, but did make some mistakes.

One mistake of note was at an auction in Kentucky. This may sound like I'm making it up but it is the honest truth. My wife always instructed me to wait until the bidding started before I got into the game. At this particular sale the auctioneer was trying to move a large lady's hat with a big white feather on one side. This type of hat had long since gone out of style. It was a rather cold day and I had worn a top coat. As the morning became warmer, I decided to carry the coat and in the process of taking it off I made some sort of gesture which the auctioneer interpreted as a bid. I became the proud owner of this lady's hat and received some funny looks from a few of the onlookers. "You buy the craziest things!" my wife and instructor said. She, on the other hand, bid in a beautiful bronze statuette for a "little bit of nothing" which later sold for a nice profit. This balanced out my "crazy" acquisition.

Another lesson she tried to teach me was to buy something early after the auction started so that the auctioneer would remember me later in the day. As a result of this instruction, I bought an item at a Maryland auction which was just as strange as the hat I had acquired in Kentucky. In fact, when I bid on this item I didn't even know what it was. The thing was a bit larger than the oval copper tubs we see so often, had churn-like paddles inside and a large crank and gears outside. "I know this is not a churn", I told my wife, "but just what is it?" She had no idea either. My teacher then remarked, "This is a new step up in your buyer's training. Before, you just bought worthless things and now you buy mysterious things." We requested an answer from an expert standing by and he informed us this was an old kitchen sized wash machine, run by hand, and used by housewives to wash small items such as hankerchiefs, napkins, small window curtains, washcloths and an occasional white shirt when there was an emergent need for one. We needed this piece of equipment in the worst way.

My wife bought a number of items at one auction in a lot. All the items in the lot were placed on a rug which was dirty and dusty from the trampling of many feet. To our surprise, there were those who wanted to buy it from us, immediately after my wife had "bid it in". It was worth buying the entire lot for a rug. The rest of the items were second-rate. After cleaning and closer examination we found it was, indeed, a fine old oriental rug. Once in awhile we get lucky. Having established my identity with the auctioneer by purchasing the washing machine, I spotted an Edison phonograph and decided I would "bid it in". I stood right beside the phonograph and patiently awaited the arrival of the auctioneer. When the bidding started I whistled, waved my arms and did everything but stand on my head to attract his attention. He was going so fast he didn't even look at me and I don't think he wanted to look at me. "So much for your theory of recognition", I later informed my tutor.

Sometime later, to heal the wound of being ignored, I "bid in" a set of wooden shafted golf clubs; a good buy! "These were what I wanted anyway", I told my mentor. "You are improving some", she said. So we acquired a rug, a washing machine and golf clubs the very same day! Also, the food at this sale was superb.

REPRODUCTIONS—TO HAVE THEM OR HAVE THEM NOT

In the old days, "repros", as they are referred to by those who recognize them, were rarely exhibited and those that were on display were so cleverly done that recognition was very difficult. More recently, most of them can be picked out readily by everyone. In consideration of those customers who cannot recognize them, we have always been honest with the unfamiliar items. One dealer informed me, "I tell a customer an item is a reproduction only if they ask me about it." We can't even abide with this idea. Why have your business ruined for the sake of one lie? Word of mouth is the best advertising mode in existence and the word travels swiftly if a customer decides to tell the world you cheated him. Some shops set aside a room or area clearly marked REPRO-DUCTIONS. One large shop in Pennsylvania advertises repro-ductions only. Some antique warehouses we have visited have them set aside in separate areas or plainly marked REPRODUC-TIONS, to aid the customer.

One of the factors leading to the mass emergence of reproduc-tions was the change in attitude of antique dealers and customers. Individuals are no longer willing to sell their antiques for "little or nothing" or give them away. Also, the customer is better edu-cated as to antique values. There are no more fifty-cent items at antique auctions. In addition, owners of antiques tend to retain them for family or keep them until they can receive the price THEY want for the item. Due to current high prices of antiques, customers have leaned more toward a good reproduction of an item than in the past. One warehouse dealer told me, "Had you come here twenty-five years ago, you would have found no repro-ductions in the building."

One of the first reproductions we encountered was a copy of the old hotel type washstand which we saw in another dealer's shop. Being raw recruits, we had him order six for our place. It had four legs, a base to set a pitcher, a round frame about waist high to set a bowl, two extensions higher up to frame a round or square mirror and two small candle holders on each side. When they were set properly in a room of a shop with candles burning, they presented a soft comfortable light and had a striking appearance. Considering the high cost of a legitimate antique pitcher and bowl set, replicas of these were available as well. We sold many of them in our shop but used them at shows only to display authentic antique pitcher and bowl sets. One customer asked my wife, "How can you sell that stand and washing set at such a low price?" She replied, "If the stand and the set were authentic antiques, they'd be in a museum, not here." We witnessed an eighteenth century washstand sell at auction for seven hundred and fifty dollars and considered it a very reasonable price.

Another reproduction seen often is "the bird in the guilded cage". These are cages of various sizes which house one or two, sometimes three brightly painted birds. The cages and birds are beautifully decorated and manufactured along the principles of the music box. When switched on, the birds chirp, turn and their little beaks open and close. We were fortunate to obtain an authentic one. It had some deficiencies but I knew a music box expert who had a personal collection of these birds and took ours to him for repairs. Apparently one part, elastic in nature, was broken so my expert cut a section from a surgical glove and made the new part. The artificial bird chirped merrily and we departed. After driving about thirty miles, we tried it again and it chirped not. We did a fast return back to my expert who, once again, restored the bird to health. "I'm sorry to bother you with this again', I said. "No problem", he replied, "I usually guarantee my work beyond a thirty mile limit". When we sold it, the bird was still chirping merrily and the lady who bought it thinks as much of it as a live one.

"Repros" of antique clocks sell rather well and the ones we stocked for our shop were well made and very reliable. We never had a clock returned to us for repairs or for poor performance. We did, however, have an unusual experience with what is called a "Dutch Wag Clock". They have a very small container which holds the spring and machinery but the pendulum is quite large, very long and decorative. Even the "repros", which are smaller, have a rather long pendulum. An authentic "Wag Clock" might cover the entire height of a wall, since they are much larger than the imitations. A friend of ours owned one and disconnected it at night because the chimes were so loud. We picked up an imitation one for our shop and couldn't get it to run properly. We did manage to sell it without having it repaired. The man who bought it told me, "I don't care if it runs or not. I'm just going to hang it on the wall of my den and look at it." Everyone has their own thing, I guess.

We bought two "repro" display cases for small jewelry and surprisingly we sold them right away. We had bought these as a result of a humorous mistake I had made. Our neighboring dealer sold old coins and jewelry and naturally had many display cases of all sizes. My wife had bought some items of jewelry and we had no case so she borrowed one from our friend until ours arrived from the warehouse. He loaned her a nice one, about two by three feet with a glass top. We kept it much longer than had been expected and when a customer admired it one day I obliged her by selling it to her. She left our place and walked by our friend next door who was sitting outside of his shop. "Where did you get that display case, lady?", he asked. "I just bought it from the man next door", she answered. "You can't have it", he informed her, "it's mine. I loaned it to that fool!" After we got the whole thing straightened out he told me, "I'd of let her have it but you didn't even get a decent price for it. How do you stay in business?"

We had absolutely no luck with "repro" easels. Having some very good antique paintings and some Maxwell Parrish prints, we needed some easels for shows. We tried three types. The first was a tripod-type, all metal, brass in color and was erected with fancy nuts and bolts. They constantly fell apart and we were constantly losing the screws. We don't recommend them. The next was another tripod type, made of wood with wooden knobs which held the thing together. Same problem; they fell, broke and when glued together fell apart again. We don't recommend this type either.

The third type was similar to the first two but much more ornate and seemed to be more structurally stable. One fell and broke and the other was damaged in transport. This was the last straw. We now just simply hang our pictures as the cooperage rate is practically nil with this method. We had one wooden type left to which a customer was attracted. My wife gave it to him. "Go ahead and take it", she told the man, "and good luck!"

THE STREET SHOW—A FUN THING

We received a contract for a one day outdoor show a few years back and decided to try this variety of exhibiting, out of curiosity more than anything else. The fee was reasonable and the show was six hours in duration. The travel to the showplace would take about six hours which removed the necessity of an overnight stay. Preparing for an outside show differs considerably from arranging for the usual inside, three day affair. Some new approaches to this show had to be considered.

First, what types of merchandise do we load into our vehicle? We decided to leave most of our classical furniture behind because of the possibility of rain. There was no rain date as the contract read, "rain or shine". We decided to take a lot of small things including some glass, pictures, some phonograph records and furniture that could withstand a bit of rain without being ruined.

We needed a large display table and I borrowed one from one of the fraternal organizations of which I am a member. This was the first mistake. While it folded and did not require much space in the van, it weighed a ton. My wife and I had a lovely time hoisting it in and out of the van and setting it up on the ground. "next time we set the glass on top of the van or on the ground or something", was her evaluation of the table. One thing we advise our friends of, concerning outside shows, is that there are no porters, unless a friendly dealer near you is willing to "pitch in" with some help.

This first outside show was in a city park which could accommodate some one hundred vans or trucks. The show was held during August and with very hot weather a factor, some sort of shelter from the sun was a must. We bought a cheap piece of tarpaulin about six foot square to fasten to the side or back door of the van. After it was erected, it appeared to be the size of a postage stamp and provided even less shade. I had a large golf umbrella in the van and I fastened this to the back of a beach chair. One of the other dealers at the show, whom we had known previously, commented, "You look like an Ethiopian Potentate sitting there." My thought was more along the line of "any port in a storm".

Our total sales during the morning consisted of three old golf clubs I had brought along and an aged butter churn. We were beginning to wonder about the value of a one day show. Being Sunday and despite the heat of the day, a huge crowd was moving into this show now that Church hours had been concluded. The dealer across from us lucked out and parked under a shade tree and we took turns going to this retreat from the sun during the course of the day. The last three hours of the show, things took a turn for the better and we found that in a few short hours we had sold more merchandise than we had in the last three weeks at our shop. My wife stated, as did the other first-timers, that there was a value in a one day outside show. "Not only that", I said, "everybody gets a nice sun tan to go along with it. Think how healthy we'll all look to the folks back home."

Our next "one-dayer" was of the street fair variety. The show-place was a resort village on the Chesapeake Bay. Upon entering the city limits, a sign read, "COME TO OUR FESTIVAL AND HAVE A BALL!" At this show, the spaces were cramped, so we had to unload our wares and then search for a place to park our vehicle. After parking, then walking back to our "spot", I passed the city limits sign again. The crowd was tremendous and we had high hopes of a productive afternoon. It was also another antique village and I was reminded of an old saying that warned of "carrying coals to Newcastle".

The booths or spaces were intermingled with all sorts of concession stands selling funnel cakes, popcorn, peanuts, candy, cotton candy, Lemonade, soft drinks, barbeque, hot dogs, hamburgers, seafood, Chinese food, chicken, and many, many types of Shish-ke-bobs. There were, in addition, a few fine year-round restaurants. If you came to eat, this was the place. If you came to drink, this was the place as well, and "the grape" in all forms was flowing like the incoming tide. Many of the attendees were walking down the streets on unsteady legs. Fortunately for us, there was a canopy in front of the antique shop and we had shade throughout the day. For some time sales were slow so we took turns walking and sampling the "goodies" available plus observing some of the other transactions taking place. One concession doing quite well, was a lady painting on children's faces. The kids were "eating it up". One street down from our booth was the bayside and many people were walking, swimming or fishing. "Next year we'll have to bring the fishing rods and at least catch some fish; we're not catching any customers", I commented.

Later in the day, we sold a phonograph and some records, a rather unusual sale for a street show but a welcome one. The passers-by had enjoyed listening to the music all day long.

At all shows, inside or outside, something unusual happens and this one was no exception. A young man who had apparently "been to the well" a number of times, spotted a stationary rocking chair which we had on display and sat down on it. I jokingly said, "If you're going to sit in the chair, you have to buy it. That's the rule here." He muttered something incomprehensible. I searched for my wife and having found her said, "Talk to the guy in the chair. I can't understand him." Besides, I was getting hungry again and walked off to find some shish-ke-bob and a cold one. When I returned the man was still sitting comfortably in the rocker—asleep! My wife said, "He bought the chair so let him sleep."

As we loaded our van and departed that evening, he was still there, resting and at peace with the world. We were only about forty five miles from home and returned there at mid-evening. At nine-thirty the phone rang and I answered it. "This is Bill from Bill's Antiques", the voice said. "You had a "spot" in front of my place at the fair today. The man who bought the rocker from you brought it in here with his receipt. That's how I got your phone number. He's sort of under the weather and wants it delivered tomorrow. He told me he came to the fair today on a motorcycle." I told Bill, "I hope the motorcycle knew the way back home!" Ah well, the sale's the thing. Right?

SHOW NEWS—NEVER PUBLISHED

One of the interesting aspects of the antique world is going into a new show at a new location. Dealers you know, who have been there before, can't tell you exactly what will transpire. Such a show took place in a Southern city. It was a rather long drive and since my wife and I both drove a van, there was little or no break at the wheel. We arrived rather tired, to begin with, and cast a doubtful eye upon the edifice in which the show was to take place. My wife said, with no disrespect to the city, "I think this is one building Grant missed when he came through here."

This was not a move-in where you could drive in on the show floor, thus we had to use our dolly. I found a porter and we began to move things into the building. This place had been a boxing and basketball arena, in ancient times, from its appearance. The basketball portion had been a nice hardwood floor at one time. Now it was scuffed, cut and more or less deteriorated. The bordering floor around it was concrete, cracked with some large chunks missing. After we had moved a few items, it began to rain. Soon we were trying to move large items of antique furniture through mud which clogged the small wheels of the dolly. We had a problem trying to keep the merchandise dry, as well. My porter said, "Good luck follows you, doesn't it." I smiled to keep from weeping.

Naturally, after we had everything inside the building, the rain ceased. We spent the remainder of the day arranging our booth. Across the way, another dealer and his wife who later became our friends, set up on concrete. They had not brought a rug and the concrete did nothing for their fine furniture.

We then withdrew to our motel, not far away, and relaxed for the evening. The rain returned, so we had dinner, watched some television, and being "bushed", retired early. Awaking the next morning, I opened the curtains of our room and saw it was raining very hard now. I informed my wife, "The monsoons have come early this year." We had a leisurely breakfast as we could not get into the show building until ten o'clock. We drove to the show, parked our vehicle and while walking through the rain witnessed a startling scene. Men were rolling fifty-five gallon cans, filled with water, OUT OF THE BUILDING! "Looks like a water pipe must have broken", I thought out loud. "I certainly hope you're right", my wife said. With that comment my nerves sent a message to my head. "The roof is leaking", I thought. "Oh Lord, I hope I'm wrong", I thought further. I was not wrong. The water was coming through the roof faster than the men could catch it and carry it out.

Fortunately, neither my booth nor the one across the way were affected but some of the other poor souls had valuable merchandise damaged or destroyed. Our friends across the way had a stream running back of their booth in the depressed concrete. A young boy with his bathtub boat could have "had a ball" here because the boat would have floated the full length of the building and out the back door. My wife said, "You don't suppose the great flood has started again, do you?" I thought there was a possibility as the rain had not diminished one little bit. I also thought that the owner of the building was either bankrupt or didn't come around to see it very often. We expressed our sympathy to those most affected by the leaking roof, but their general attitude was "win some, lose some." We developed a great deal of steadfastness over the years from people like these.

Things dried up on the next day but on the final day of the show we moved out in rain one more time. The porters moved more water than merchandise. We sold one lamp. The dealer next to me sold a bundle of new chicken coops, which people for something or another need. I resolved, that on returning home, I would build a few of them out in the shed for future shows. Regardless of the outcome, learning takes place at all shows.

At another "first time" show, we encountered more challenges, however the weather was not a problem this time. The arrangement of the show was the problem. This show was held at a Church, fortunately not far from home. When we arrived at the show, we found that the young men of the Church were off someplace, playing baseball that day; thus no porters. My wife and I were amazed at the remaining strength stored up in our bodies at our advanced ages. There was an average size social room in the church, where some of the dealers were located. Other spaces were in the hallways and Sunday School rooms, some on the second floor and some in the basement. Movement of merchandise was either up or down. We had a basement room and going down there was a ninety degree turn on the steps and another at the bottom going into the room. We had one huge couch to move and you should have seen these two ageing dealers handling the baby down the stairs.

The other items were easily moved and we set it up as a living room, rug and all. It looked nice and included an old Atwater-Kent radio. "The Cadillac of radios", in its day, and it played good music from Washington, D.C. stations all day long.

All the parishioners and guests thought it was a beautiful room; they said so and then went upstairs to eat. One positive factor of a Church show is the excellent food. I said, "This isn't a Church show, it's a Church social." My wife agreed and informed me she had been up twice to eat and the food was great. I tried some of the great food, enjoyed it and while I was away, Adaline sold the radio. After that sale, the people just passed through, either before or after eating. I thought of putting my sign up which read, MUSEUM $5.00 ENTRANCE FEE. With the sale of the radio, minus the food cost, minus the rent we still came out ahead but the Church was the big winner on this one and there's nothing wrong with that. After back to back shows of an adverse nature, we adopted the old postal service motto: "Neither rain, snow, sleet nor darkness or night will deter us in making our appointed rounds".

A new pleasant experience came about at a large convention center show. One dealer had an excellent pewter collection and the lady dealer next to him had a great collection of silver and table settings. Our booth was directly across from them with furniture, some paintings and a phonograph. At dinner time, the pewter man went to a Chinese restaurant and came back with enough for all. The lady set one of our tables with a nice table cloth and settings. At dinner time, the pewter man was in place. Table set in proper style, we lit the candles, I put on some Victor solon music and we were in business. "Bon appetit", said my French speaking wife.

MOVING IN—THE JOY OF IT

Moving into an antique show can be an endurance trial or an easy procedure, depending on some variables such as vehicle space, access to entrances, weather, attitude of the promoter and

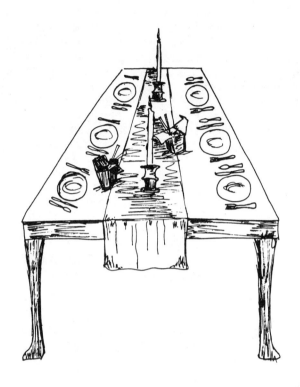

the agility of porters. One factor we can always count on is that it is interesting. Regardless of the particular experience and while the hard work of the move-in may be unpleasant, later we talk about it and have a laugh or two. Humor is the anecdote of remorse, especially in the antique world. I remember a few incidents that my wife and I shared moving into antique shows.

In the early days of our experience, we had been loading our merchandise in a van and a station wagon but for a large show at a convention center we decided to rent a trailer for additional items, should they be needed. We had been advised as to the approach to the center by the promoter but when I arrived with the station wagon and trailer I made a wrong turn and ended up in a business office parking lot next to the center. I would like to advise my dealer friends, at this time, that it takes nearly an hour to turn a station wagon and trailer around in a small, crowded parking lot. The price of renting a trailer is not worth the corresponding rise in one's blood pressure.

Having emerged victorious from this odd experience, I approached Step 2 in trying the enter the convention center. I drove around the block and parked my assemblage in the proper line, about 54th in sequence. Eventually I reached the entrance ramp to the show. Our preliminary instructions read, "We will tell you when to come up the ramp". The security guard outside, armed with a walkie-talkie in hand, said "Go up the ramp", which I did. The promoter stood at the top of the ramp, walkie-talkie in hand, red in the face, shouting, "Who told you to come up the ramp!? You are one hour late and out of line!" I replied sheepishly, "The security guard told me to come up". "Well, I run the show; he doesn't", he growled, "You pull that thing over to the left and I'll try to straighten out this mess!" As I pulled to the left, a lady dealer arranging her merchandise yelled. "You hit that table and I'll give you trouble!" I answered, "Lady, after what I've just been through, if you think you can give me trouble you must be a creative genius."

Finally, the disgruntled promoter directed me down the proper aisle to our booth. There were dealers on both sides of the aisle, busily preparing the booths and as I wavered the station wagon and trailer through this maze, they stared at me with frightened eyes, some as big as saucers.

As I approached our booth, my wife glared at me with a look of disdain that would have put the promoter's rage to shame. All the merchandise from the van, which she had driven, had been unloaded an hour earlier and had been pushed to one side. "Where have you been?", she asked, "I couldn't do a thing until the rug arrived and it's in the station wagon. I'll bet you stopped for a drink somewhere." By this time I had just about reached my "boiling point", and replied, "No dear, but what a great idea!"

To remove the rug, the porter and I had to unhitch the trailer, not an easy task when the trailer is loaded, plus detaching all the cables and electric connections. The porter sort of grunted and told me I should have packed the rug last in the back of the van, since it was to be the first item to be unloaded. Ah! A new traffic management expert on the horizon. He was right, of course, but by this time my nerves were wearing rather thin at the edges. While struggling with the trailer, the hyper voice of the promoter was heard from the loudspeaker system. "One of the dealers has already violated our moving-in rules!, he exclaimed, "and the next time any dealer does not follow directions, they will be excluded from our future shows!" The porter and I continued to unload that station wagon and trailer and a thought came to me. If it were not for the fact that we had a beautiful room across the street, if there were not a cool bar and a cozy restaurant where I could escape my tormentors, I might apply for exclusion from future shows at this very time.

We did have a lovely weekend and over the course of the show, did quite well. But, to further the animosity of the promoter, the television people he had scheduled gave coverage to our booth instead of some of the ones he had picked out. We made some sales as a result of this coverage. As our punishment, at load-out time, our vehicles were called at the very last. But we had the last laugh. As all the other vehicles were gone, I had no trouble maneuvering the station wagon and trailer. We arrived back home a little later than usual but successful.

At another show in another city a new array of challenges faced us when moving in. The show was in the ballroom on the lower level of a one thousand room hotel, potentially a great location. When we arrived, we were told there were three entry points. The first was a long ramp descending from ground level at a forty-five degree angle. My wife, Adaline, said "I wouldn't back down there if I were Evil Kneivel." Other dealers observed it with terror in their eyes. The second was from the front of the motel, through the main entrance, thence down an escalator to the ballroom level. This was not conducive to moving large furniture, which we were going to exhibit. Even the glass dealers looked upon it with frightful doubt, considering the value of their merchandise. We chose the third alternative which was to back the vehicles up to the kitchen ramp which was about five feet high, thence by dolly through the kitchen to the hallway and then by elevator down to the ballroom.

We hired the help of a young giant who I suspected played tackle for one of the local football teams. With his strength, our patience and careful handling of large items, we succeeded, in spite of a never-ending arrival and departure of garbage and delivery trucks, in unloading our merchandise. This took nearly six hours because about forty other dealers were involved and only two vehicles could park at the ramp at one time. Refreshing, however, was the many questions we answered for the cooks and kitchen help about our antiques. While they admired our vocation, as we worked through the day, we became very hungry and our admiration for their vocation became stronger for their's. I vowed that on our departure we would risk the ramp rather than take the culinary route. Thank Heaven I know longer use a trailer. It would have been enough to draw tears from the eyes of the most calloused veteran.

We were not very sophisticated in those days as compared to the professional dealers. They had fancy packing cases with their business name and address on them and nice blue wrappings for their glassware. We used empty whiskey cartons and newspapers. As the two professionals next to us calmly unwrapped their expensive glassware, I occasionally caught them glancing at our amateurish ways and means. As the show wore on we became friends and at dinner one evening they were grinning at us. I asked the cause of their mirth and one told us, "We decided, after watching you move in and unpack, to call you 'Laura and Hardy'." H! Ha! Ha!.

How many strange things can happen at a show? Upon arriving at this particular show I discovered I had one pair of dress shoes and no work shoes. The dress shoes were a bit small at that. After two days they were beginning to hurt a bit. I told my wife, "I've got to find another pair of comfortable shoes somewhere because my feet are killing me!" Being Sunday, I found about everything but a shoe store and returned, empty handed, to the show.

On departure, even though we used the treacherous ramp, the loading was slow and we returned home late at night. Regardless of our problems, we had a nice show, made some new friends, and even now when we run into old friends, we are still known as "Laura and Hardy". After we were home and had been refreshed, my wife asked, "It wasn't so bad after all, was it?" "No, I said, "but my FEET SURE HURT!"

MOVING OUT—ANOTHER JOY

If you watched a move-out exercise at the close of an antique show you would wonder what happened to all the nice people you

met while the show was in progress. At move-out time, the smiling, talkative dealer you bought a vase from has turned into a red-faced nervous wreck. The courteous, helpful and observing promoter and his staff turn into a group of efficiency experts in a hurry to get home, get you out of the building and on your way home; the sooner the better. Both parties, in a hurry, make mistakes and clash. The conflict reminds me of a line from a Matthew Arnold poem, "Dover Beach", which reads, "And life is like on a darkling plain where ignorant armies clash by night". This line does not present a pretty picture but then neither does the mass exodus from an antique show. My compliments go to the old professionals who calmly pack their merchandise, take their time, don't break things and sort of tolerate the others who are unsystematically fighting windmills.

At a large show in a large hotel we suspected the worst from the start because when we arrived there was no one supervising the load-in procedure. "This is not a good thing", my daughter remarked. She was right and it was much worse at load-out time. There was a small ramp in the back of the hotel which could accommodate five or six large vehicles and the parking area for those dealers waiting to unload was jammed. The trucks were just "milling around", trying not to run into each other.

On Sunday, the move-out day, the dealer across from us had a startling experience. He was a linen dealer from New Hampshire and we had exchanged pleasantries during the show. On this closing afternoon, he asked me to watch his booth while he went to the show office to pick up load-out information. When he returned he looked shaken. "You won't believe what the promoter just told me", he said nervously, "She said she was getting too old to worry about things like that! What are we going to do!?, he said. "Struggle out like we struggled in, I guess?", I replied.

You would have not had to watch TV that evening to get a good laugh; you could have come to this show and watched us move out. As the promoter had previously announced, there was no move-out plan. In addition, the porters were Union regulated and dispersed by their foreman; the dealer had no selection. I guess there was nothing wrong with this except this group had no experience in handling antiques. This can be dangerous and expensive.

The last trucks to unload on Friday, just left the trucks in place and of course, they were the first to load-out. The rest of us had to suffice by maneuvering and having a little luck. Thank Heavens my wife and daughter were there to help handle our merchandise. My daughter managed to move our small station wagon into an early position and then, guess what else happened? It started to rain.

We saw a highboy, very expensive, dropped off the ramp, a four foot drop. Needless to say, it became a lowboy, in dire need of extensive repair. The amateur porters were having a field day. Fortunately, we survived with all our merchandise; a bit rain-soaked as well as ourselves and otherwise, it was a good day. My wife became lost in the city with the station wagon but finally found her way home. In spite of all the hazards of the day, we could still smile as we had a very good show.

Some promoters do not realize that we senior citizens are not as spritely as we used to be, don't move as fast as we used to move and have lost some of our strength. Even if we have a good porter, we slow him down. On the positive side, we like to load our valuable merchandise carefully so that it arrives securely back at the shop. Some promoters hire another person to supervise the loading processes which is fine until that person gets the idea he is all-important and untouchable. Some forget that they are working for us, since we all help pay their salaries. The dealers who were held in high esteem during the show, exhibiting fine merchandise and arranging their booths attractively, suddenly become to the load-master, vagabond trash who should exit swiftly and get on back to where they came from. Schizophrenia does not limit itself to any particular vocation. It is evident in all walks of life, including the antique profession.

At another show I was told by the "Simon Legree" of the day that I was too slow and to "hurry it up!" "What's the matter? Are you slow or is he (the porter) slow?", he blurted out. We were slow because we were both the same age, sixty-four. I asked him who assigned the porters and he informed me that he was that man. I remarked, "Next time send me a younger man and don't talk so much, you're holding us up!" The porter and I exchanged a grin as this important personage stomped away to harass someone else. The same man told my wife later she had ten minutes to move the small station wagon. She informed him, "It takes that long to start it. What's the hurry? Is there a sale at a dime store you want to attend?" We told the promoter what we thought of their efficiency expert as did several other dealers and after that show we never saw him again.

To clear the air, let me say that promoters who tolerate these things from their employee or "loading supervisor" are in the minimum. The real professional promoters hire qualified people who enhance the show and help you in and out of a show properly. Also, not ALL move-out experiences are bad ones.

We had four glass supports we used to hold up glass shelving. They were nicely shaped and had a striking design on them. We really didn't think they were made for the purpose of separating shelves. People had wanted to buy them separately or singly but we held on to them for our purposes. On leaving a big show, we left them in a packing box beside one of the vans. At the same show, six months later, a dealer approached us with our box. Our name was stamped on the side. "We would have gotten them to you sooner, but we just found it with our things", he said.

We were happy that we had marked our packing boxes and that there were so many honest people in the antique business. This off-sets some of the harassment we experience from time to time. All's well that ends well.

DELIVERIES—THE FUN AND THE BACKACHES

We have always made it a policy to deliver to our customers, free of charge, if within a reasonable distance. It is a good business procedure and promoters like it as well as dealers. In fact, some promoters like it as well as dealers to the extent that they have a delivery service available at their shows but their agent charges for it. Sometimes it is worth using this service and paying for it to eliminate the backache. Usually, I have a porter help me load an item for delivery and there is normally some help at the other end. Before she married, my daughter used to help me a lot and she was an able assistant. She was strong and knew how to handle valuable antiques. She walked into one of our shows and when she looked at me she remarked, "I know. You made a sale. How do I know? Because you have a smile on your face, you said, 'Hello Honey', we have a delivery to make and it's raining."

One of the first deliveries I made by myself caused me to question the wisdom of doing this for free in the future. While exhibiting at a large city Convention Center, a man purchased a considerable amount of merchandise and wanted it delivered that evening. It was already dark at seven o'clock as it always is in November. I told my wife I probably would not be back in time for closing, but would make the delivery. The customer lived about five miles from the Convention Center. The delivery was easy. Another dealer across from us helped me load the merchandise and I merely had to follow my buyer to his home. On arrival, I discovered ten steps up to the walkway leading to the house, and then ten more up to the front door. This was not an ordinary residence; more like an estate.

Steps are the terrors of delivery service. The gentleman buyer

and I negotiated all these and, thank Heavens, the items were placed downstairs. This being done he said, "I saw a nice hunt board (server) in your booth. Would you mind going back to get it? If it looks good here in the house, I'll buy it." I told him I could do it tomorrow but not this night. It was beginning to rain and I don't see very well at night when it's raining. He informed me they would not be at home tomorrow so I probably lost a sale. I couldn't have gotten back that night anyway because when leaving I made the wrong turn and toured the city for a couple of hours before I arrived back at the hotel. My wife thought I had stopped at a bar and I wish I had. I could have rested my tired eyes from the glare of the street and wet windshield for a few minutes.

When we do shows in large cities we often meet those who live in mansions, and mansions, as big as they are, sometimes are hard to find. At a large convention center show in another city, a man listened to one record played on one of my phonographs and said, "I'll take it." No fuss, no strain, no bargaining; a lovely sale. He gave me an address of 2 Bradley Boulevard where it was to be delivered. Leaving an hour later, I finally found Bradley Boulevard and noted a large apartment complex on the right. There was every number there you could think of but 2. Then I saw a huge castle type building across the street. *This* was number 2. I drove into the circular tree-lined driveway and discreetly parked in the rear, near the kitchen entrance. A house servant in dark trousers and a white kitchen jacket exited and helped me carry the phonograph to the huge dining hall.

This was the type of dining hall you see in the movies with a monstrous fireplace, long table to seat about thirty people, a great chandelier; the works. His wife passed through the room long enough to grumble about his buying useless things and kept walking. The buyer didn't answer as I don't think he even noticed she was in the room, he being so interested in his new purchase. He walked across the room and returned with four records. They had been recorded by the "Two Black Crows", a comedy team of the old phonograph age. He thanked me and as I left he and the servant were listening to one of the records and laughing together; a rich man with an ordinary taste in humor.

Our favorite delivery was to a couple living in the Newburg, New York area. After making a delivery in Virginia, I called

100

back to the shop to see what was happening and let my wife know I was starting back. She said excitedly, "A couple from New York bought our three-piece parlor set. The man rented a U-Haul trailer to take the set back but he has a foreign car of some sort and the trailer won't fasten to the bumper. What shall we do?" "I'll tell you what we'll do", I answered, "For the money he paid for that set, I'll take it to New York for a couple of tanks of gas. Chris can help." "That's a long trip", she replied, "are you sure you want to do that?" I assured her I did as it was only an eight hour drive, my daughter loved to drive and take a trip and it would be easy with two drivers. We left early on Tuesday and arrived at the buyer's home in the afternoon, eight hours on the "button" with only one food stop.

This couple were restoring an old home in the affluent area and the parlor set fitted right in. It was near Rheinbeck, NY and the homes of Loretta Switt and James Cagney. People talk about Southern hospitality but my daughter and I sampled some Northern hospitality that evening. When we mentioned we had to find lodging for the night, they insisted we stay there; they also served us dinner and the gentleman and I watched a football game later. The next morning they served us breakfast and gave me a travel check to return home; all this for just making a delivery.

On the way back we stopped early at a good motel, had dinner and relaxed. On checking out the next day, I thought the bill was exorbitant and asked the desk clerk for an explanation. He asked me to take note of the TV movie charges. I looked at my daughter and her eyes were mere slits; it's a wonder she could even see. She had stayed up all night and watched ALL the movies on the schedule. "You certainly know how to eat up all the profits", I remarked. She replied, "Not only that, you'll have to drive the rest of the way home. I'm sleepy." Oh well, good help is hard to find.

PACKING AND MOVING—A COLLATERAL TRADE

Years ago, my wife's mother decided to come to Maryland and abide with us. She had a small home in Kentucky and this small home was full of possessions. She and my wife had a tendency to "hold on" to things and what we classify as possessions sometimes translate to "clutter". My son and I rented a U-Haul truck and with my wife driving the station wagon, we traveled to Kentucky in order to help her mother move to Maryland.

When the time came to load, my son and I went to work with the will but did not know the way to load a truck. Soon we had the floor of the truck covered with items but discovered we had loaded only one room of furniture. This is when we discovered my wife's ability to pack twenty items into a ten item space. She instructed us how to stack things and arrange them and we soon concluded that we would, in fact, be able to load everything in the house into this truck. We succeeded! I wondered where my wife had picked up this talent for loading but after living twenty years with her mother and rearranging our home several hundred times, I began to understand. I thought my wife had experience in packing and it surely came in handy when we started our antique business. I told another lady dealer how good my wife was at packing and she told me, "You think she's good? I found sixteen chairs at a flea market and packed them all in the back seat of my car!" I agreed that she also had great talent in this field of endeavor.

As to general experience, we had survived four stateside moves and two overseas tours while in the Army. Our first move was to Germany immediately after our marriage. This one was a "snap". All we possessed were our clothes an my bride had packed a pressing iron for her good dresses and a couple of my white shirts. On leave and on our way traveling to Europe we acquired more clothes and other items. When we arrived at Bremerhaven, Germany, we discovered that there would now be a problem packing everything; I rolled everything Army style in order to get all our clothes into one duffle bag. Watching me, my bride exclaimed, "What are you doing with my good dresses?!" I explained, "Things take up less space when they are rolled". She allowed that they would not look so good when they were unrolled and she was right. She had shown true brilliance in bringing the iron.

All in all, this was the easiest move we ever made. All the big moves, later on, were handled either by German or American professionals. In all our transfers through the years, only one

piece of furniture was damaged. In spite of these experts' ability, my wife always insisted on seeing every item packed and unpacked. I suppose she picked up a world of packing knowledge this way as well, but for myself, I preferred to retreat to the club or the Gasthous and leave the problems to the "pro's".

I forgot to mention that my mother-in-law operated a small Pekingese kennel and during two of our moves, not overseas of course, we had to deal with nine dogs. Try this out on your patient and understanding nature some time.

The first antique show we moved into required more planning and arranging than we had bargained for, in spite of all the household moves we had made. Moving in and out of shows now requires about two hours, whereas in the early days this was a six hour effort. Of course, at the first show we packed everything backwards and left behind, at the shop, some items we needed. Our first booth was a shambles but with experience things started to look more presentable. Fortunately, at this first show we were not far from the shop and could return for items left behind.

One amazing feature of our first show as that it seemed we took more things back to the shop than we had brought with us. One old experienced dealer told us, "This is normal. Many times more things come out of a show than go in." In our case, the fascination with the first show and the attractive way the old "pro's" set up their booths led to new acquisitions on our part. We developed an attitude of, "If we sell a few things, I'd like to have that nice parlor set in the booth, three down from us." We regularly followed through on these ideas until it finally dawned on us that shows were designed to sell merchandise rather than to buy it. We were not the only ones who did these things. At our first show we sold an oak folding card table to a dealer before the show opened. "I didn't even set it down on the floor!", I remarked to Adaline. At another show we sold a rug we had just put down on the floor and I had to drive back fifty miles to get another one. When I returned my partner (wife) informed me that the booth arrangement looked better without a rug. Oh! Joy!

After working a few years without porters, we either "got smart" or older and probably a combination of both. We took part in a local show where the members of the Lion's Club acted as porters and they did a conscientious job. The move, in and out, was so easily accomplished that we rarely worked without porters

My wife and I at our first show—the "No Foolin' Antique Show" in Waldorf, Maryland, in 1981—and trying to look confident.

again. I was amazed at a show in one of the large cities when a man drove our vehicles onto the floor and unloaded them for a nominal fee. He did such a good job that we actually had little arranging to do after he was finished. My wife said, "We're getting a little spoiled now."

We were always interested in the different ways other dealers managed their moving and setting up. One couple, for example, were from Long Island, NY, and they made their entire move and set up with a station wagon. They dealt exclusively in expensive glassware and their merchandise was neatly packed in boxes in the wagon. They were particularly efficient at the "drive in" type shows, being able to park their vehicle right next to their booth. They were in and out of shows in no time. I told my partner and wife, "A couple of more years and we are going into glass instead of this heavy furniture." This thought always returns to me after four hours of moving and arranging. Sometimes we get lucky on a move-in. Information concerning the set up of one show informed us that the display area would have wall to wall carpeting, thus we did not pack a rug. The carpeting was there but was a horrible color. I was stomping around, addressing the Diety because we hadn't packed a rug when our neighboring dealer told us, "I brought three oriental rugs but have a small booth and can't display them. Why don't you put them down and use them. It will help us both." We accepted his offer and our furniture was beautifully exhibited as were his rugs.

Another couple from Illinois employ a large camper for living, traveling, doing shows and packing their merchandise. They too, dealt primarily in glassware. We have enjoyed coffee and other refreshments in the van at several shows. Now this is the class approach to doing antique shows, traveling and entertaining your friends, if you can afford it.

Still another couple who run a shop, promote shows and display their merchandise as well, own a large truck which used to be used to transport blue crabs and oysters from Southern Maryland. They tell us the only disadvantage to the truck is a large crab painted on the side. Customers at the show approach the promoter and want to know who owns the truck with the big crab on the side. They want to buy crabs. "They even gather around the truck when I'm gone", the dealer informed me, "and when I return they are ready to buy crabs." "You ought to load some in the truck", I

106

told him, "and then if you have a bad show you'll have the crabs to fall back on." He's thinking about it.

There is an advantage to loading, unloading and arranging your own merchandise, at least while you're still able to do it. The thought hit me one day when my wife asked, "What will we do if the antique business fails?" "Well", I replied, "we can either go fishing, travel or just change our shop sign to read, BU-CHANAN'S, PACKING AND MOVING, EXPERIENCED AND RELIABLE.

Sales are not "booming" right now so we're thinking about it.

THE MYSTERY OF THE ISOLATED SHOW

Sometimes we do shows that appear to be "golden opportunities" for sales but just don't amount to a "hill of beans". They are not just remote incidents but happen a few times each year. What is the mystery surrounding these "phantom" shows? Poor planning? We think not. Incidents happen sometimes "out of the blue", so to speak, to ruin what might have been a great show.

Once an experienced dealer told me that he had researched market areas for years and investigated the potential of a show before he signed a contract. After awhile, he decided that he was wasting his time and just joined the rest of us gamblers. Quite a few of his ventures had just "bombed out", despite his investigations. One, for instance, was in a large midwestern city where several large manufacturing companies were located in the same area. Employment was at a high level and people were affluent. He contracted the show several months in advance after researching it and following the advice of other dealers, whose success was related to him. It was a huge show, and expertly set up but on opening day the employees of the manufacturing companies struck. They all belonged to the same union, therefore, thousands were temporarily unemployed. Employees and their families, when on strike, do not foolishly or casually. spend money. The dealer told me, "Enough of scientific research. I'll use a dart board from now on!"

Another unsuspected incident fouled up another promoter's plans. Thinking the schoolhouse would attract customers, he scheduled several antique shows in the surrounding institutions of learning. One such show in a large high school had proven to be successful. The particular show that failed took place in a moderately sized private school. The school had a fairly large student body and the parents or sponsors of these students were considered to be "well of" financially. A small show of about fifty dealers was set up with a good range of merchandise but on the first day of a two-day show, only some one hundred and fifty shoppers attended and the show closed two hours early. A mystery! On the second day, a Sunday, only about seventy five customers attended and the show closed three hours early. Poor advertising? No, on Saturday the school played football, away, of course. The dealers also found out that the parents or sponsors of the students lived in other parts of the state and some out of the state, but what happened to the thousands of people who lived in the immediate area? Who knows? The food, however, was excellent and reasonably priced as it always is at school or church shows. Our recommendations to the promoter was to schedule the next show when the football team was playing at home and arrange the show and the food concession around the periphery of the athletic field.

One very interesting show, but a failure, took place in a wealthy suburb of Philadelphia, Pa. The show was located in a very large resort hotel.

The show set-up was great as we could drive our vehicles in and unload, always a pleasure after "dollying in" most of the time. We enjoyed our week-end stay as we ate well, slept well, enjoyed the evening entertainment, but that was the end of the story. Something happened to the antique show customers. Where were they? At slow shows, conversation picks up. We met the dealers across from us and struck up a friendship that still exists. During the afternoon of the first day, I ventured across to these dealers and asked, "How are things going? I haven't sold a thing!" My friend, we will call him Ben, always in a good mood, good or bad show, replied, "I can't even get anybody to steal from me!"

What was the mystery of this flop? For one thing, an antique car show was scheduled outside for the same weekend. You would have thought some of this crowd would have rubbed off on us but there were so many people at the car show, that parking was at a minimum for antique buffs. I will say this was one of the biggest antique car shows I have ever seen and enjoyed it myself. "Which one do you want?" I asked Ben. "I couldn't even afford the gas", he answered.

A nearby junior military academy sponsors an antique show each year and the first time we tried it we were quite successful, thus we rescheduled for the next year. This was another show where good food abounded. Adaline and I have thought many times about taking up the food concession business at these shows instead of displaying antiques. The concession people never fail. This being another private school, the parents and friends of the school do the portering and operate the kitchen. We have never seen more dedicated individuals. As a private school they can also operate a bar which is a definite advantage, particularly on hot days.

The show was usually held in conjunction with an annual oyster festival, which attracts some 35,000 people. One year, the show's planning staff decided an antique show in a large city some seventy-five miles away would conflict with their show and scheduled it a week later. I, with infinite foresight, decided not to do the show because of the absence of the oyster festival. Just to make sure I was right, I attended the show the first day and found the building packing with people. I told a friend, a parent of one of the students, "I goofed this time." "Have a beer and relax", he said, "and come back next year. We'll save you a space." No mystery here. Everyone makes mistakes.

Have you ever done a show at a golf resort? DON'T! If you do, by all means take your golf clubs. This was another case of predicting the potential of a market area and failing. The resort was made up on a huge hotel with several swimming pools, inside and out, exercise rooms, riding trails, walking trails, excellent restaurants and bars, twenty-seven golf holes plus indoor and outdoor tennis courts. The show was in the indoor tennis court building and accommodated some two hundred dealers. This was a two day show, Saturday and Sunday.

The golf course abounded with golfers, the pools with swimmers, the courts with tennis players, the restaurants with diners, the bars with drinkers and the trails with walkers. The parking lots were full and no place to park for the antiquers. No mystery here! Those unpredictables again! Since this was the first show here, the promoter had not bargained for the road construction taking place on the main road in front of the resort which backed traffic up for miles. A thousand vehicles carrying week-end golfers jammed the parking lots. An antique dealer or shopper didn't have a chance but my wife said, "Wasn't it a lovely week-end?" She always sees the bright side. TENNIS ANYONE?

GAINS AND LOSSES—THE ANTIQUE EQUATION

While stationed in Kentucky, my wife and I attended a combination farm and home auction. The day was mighty cold for an auction but the company running the sale set aside a kitchen of the farm house for hot coffee and snacks during the day. Those attending looked over the items placed outside, went into the house to warm up and then came back out when the item they had an interest in came up for bidding. This being back in my truly ignorant days, everything looked like a hopeless mess to me. My wife spotted a balloon back chair and "bid it in" at a price that would appear to be ridiculous today. After it was refinished and re-upholstered, it was truly a beautiful item. We decided to keep it in our home and it still remains in our Victorian parlor today. This was one chair I didn't have to wrestle with in the restoration process. We could classify it as a plus.

Another piece of furniture for our home was a large walnut armoire or clothes press, circa 1860. My wife bought this at a sale and converted it into a display cabinet for her "pretties'. This item was structurally damaged and in pieces but she put this monster back together, refinished it and lined the inside with attractive wall paper. The solid part of the large doors were beyond repair so she had glass installed. Later, she added a miniature set of lights to show off our collection of cut glass and other interesting glass creations.

The original collection of cut glass was my mother's and the other items were ones we had found in this country and in Europe. My part of this array of glass items came to me by an act of friendship. My mother and father passed away when I was twenty years of age and I was very careless, as all young people are, with the possessions they left behind. I gave a piano to my church, some fine furniture including a china closet, which meant nothing to me, to relatives and made other typical mistakes. I sold some items recklessly.

When it came to the cut glass, other valuable glassware, family albums and silverware, my friend stepped in and preserved them from my youthful generosity and ignorance. She had been a close friend of my mother's, and understanding my unconcern at the time she advised me to let her pack these things in my mother's cedar chest and store them in her home. After my wife and I married, we traveled home and picked up the chest and contents. Our friend has passed away but my wife and I will never forget the genuinely nice thing she did for us. My wife later made snide comments about my handling of the situation when she learned how many items I had given away. A few years back, one of my cousins did return one of my grandfather's Victorian hall tables for which I am grateful. The only way I can rationalize my folly is that most of the people I know have made the same mistake. I wish I had all the old phonographs, radios, records, furniture, lightning-rods, etc., that found their way to the dump many years ago.

One big gain my wife instigated took place while I was stationed in Korea for sixteen months. There was nothing I could "mess up" on an antique transaction that far away. She and her mother traveled to Indiana and returned, having bought a square grand piano at a ridiculously low price.

Even considering the cost of having it shipped back to Kentucky, this was still a good purchase. All it needed was a little refinishing. When I returned home from Korea and saw it sitting in the parlor I had to try it, being a music lover. "It doesn't play", my wife said, "because it has to be repaired and tuned. We will have it done when we finally settle down and retire." Fifteen years later we attempted to have this done in Maryland. We found a man who repaired it, as best he could, put in some new wire and keys and tuned it. Some of the strings were quite brittle from age and continued to break under stress. We found another man who hand carved a music holder for us. This beautiful piece now sits in our parlor and can be played, but it is necessary to find sheet music that doesn't require the use of C Sharp, A Flat, D Sharp, and B Flat in varying octaves.

We have one item that can't be classified as a gain or a loss because it is valuable to me but my wife hates it with an increasingly "purple passion" as the years go by. It is a painting of a tiger, with the First Cavalry Division patch on its side; he is cross-eyed and bloated, his tongue hangs out and there are bugs flying about his head. The caption reads, *EVERY MAN A TIGER!*. I have hung it in many places in our show and our home but every time I want to show it to someone it has disappeared. My wife takes it down and hides it. Sometimes it takes days to find it again.

Another favorite of mine is a photo taken at a "Hobo Party" which the officers of my unit at Fort Knox, Kentucky, had arranged. My costume was really one of the funniest at the party and the photo was taken while I was dancing with a lady whose costume was as funny as mine. From the looks of the photo. I must have been having a good time! The Battalion Commander was having a good time, as well. I had a picture of him with a top hat on, swinging from a rafter in a huge truck tire. Hilarious! My wife hates these pictures as much as my "tiger". She really hates them because I broke a glass bowl, full of potato salad during the course of the evening. When she sees the picture, she always reminds me that I broke a valuable glass bowl. Will she never desist?

My wife has an opium pipe, a real antique, but as far as I know, she has never used it. Her father owned a building in our home town which housed a Chinese laundry. The proprietor, E. Lin Kim, thought the world of my wife as a child and during her high school years. When she left home, he gave her the old opium pipe. It is an unusual attraction and we have no idea how old it might be. It looks stranger, however, sitting around the house when we have guests, I set it aside. Sometimes, when we have a small dinner party, Adaline says, "You aren't going to show these people that ridiculous painting and those silly photos, are you?" "Not unless you show them your opium pipe", I reply.

OLD MOVIES AND PLAYS—ANTIQUE
RESEARCH

Our entire family is made up of movie buffs. My wife's father owned a movie theatre for years in Ohio and as a child, she sat in the front row and enjoyed what we now refer to as "the classical movies". In the same town, the gang of boys from my neighborhood were given ten cents each Saturday to watch a cartoon, a serial, such as *Buck Rogers,* and a double feature, usually the Western type. We were always dressed as soldiers or cowboys and carried the appropriate toy weapons. We had a talented member of our gang who could fashion toy guns out of a slab of wood so we were always well armed. The manager of the theatre always made us check our weapons at the ticket office. We loved it! I had no idea that my future wife was sitting in the front row.

During a tour of duty in Germany, while serving in the Army, our children never objected to going to the nursery while my wife and I attended social functions because the TV reception there was better than in our quarters. Before they all grew up and left home, there were TV sets stationed at various places throughout our home. No one could miss anything; this is the history of our family and the entertainment world.

After a few years in the antique world, our viewing approach to old movies began to change. We were watching a late-night "oldie", *Ah Wilderness,* a movie based on a O'Neil play. This movie starred Wallace Berry. My wife commented, "Look at that Victorian sofa. It's just like the one we sold three months ago." During the rest of the movie we set aside the drama and acting and picked out interesting items of the antique world. We had begun a whole new approach to researching antiques, the old movies. The question, "I wonder what's on TV that is interesting tonight?", now became, "What antiques will we see in the old movie tonight?"

Some outstanding examples of these types of old movies come to mind. To start with, try *Sunset Boulevard,* with Gloria Swanson and William Holden. Not only is it an outstanding movie, an Academy Award winner, but the scenes in the old Hollywood type mansion are abounding in a mind boggling array of antiques, including furniture, carpets, winding stairs, high ceilings and great costumes; the "works". My comment was primarily concerned with an enormous dining room table seating about twenty-four people. "What a party you could have around that thing!", was my thought.

If you like a good comedy from beginning to end, watch *You Can't Take It With You,* derived from the original play by Moss

113

My "Tiger." Look close enough, and you can
see the "conversation piece" opium pipe at the
bottom left.

Hart. Watch either the old one starring Lionel Barrymore and Mischa Ayer as "Kolenkov", the Russian ballet instructor or the new rendition starring Art Carney as "Grandpa". We are partial to this one as we acted in the play while stationed in Kentucky. The play was done in the small college theatre and there was so much property on the stage and so many actors on the stage at the same time, the local reviewer made an accurate report. "There was so much of a traffic jam on the stage, I'm surprised no one fell off and hurt themselves." From the antique standpoint, it is a feast to behold; old lamps, old furniture, an old bird cage, old kitchenware, and an old desk and typewriter plus costumes out of the late twenties. Old curtains and drapes were also on display.

I was cast as "Kolenkov", the ballet teacher and Adaline had the role of "The Grand Duchess, Olga Katerina". We practiced our lines for weeks and after the play had been performed, we discovered we were still speaking with an accent. We talked with the man who played "Kolenkov" recently in a local production of the play and he was still saying, "Vel, my friend, you like it, eh?" Or he would say, "Ave a trink?" If you watch this one, take particular note of the music, costumes, and the old phonograph.

Here are a few more references should these "oldies" appear on your TV schedules. For a view of the ladies' fur coat and hat styles of the late twenties see Bette Davis in *Dark Victory*. For European Victorian and Empire furniture with clothing styles see *The Razor's Edge* with Tyrone Power and Jean Tierney taken from a W. Somerset Maugham book; also the old *A Farewell To Arms* with Gary Cooper from a Hemingway classic. For rustic Tennessee style dress and furniture watch Gary Cooper in *Sergeant York*. For old American western style clothing and farm environment, *How The West Was Won, starring James Stewart and a cast of hundreds is great. While on the subject of this great actor, also try to see Bell, Book And Candle*. In this one, the female lead, Kim Novak, operated an antique shop with many interesting items on display.

Have you ever watched any of the old Marx Brothers movies with Margaret Dumont? *A Night At The Opera* is full of great costumes of the day and Victorian furniture. You can also enjoy the singing of Alan Jones and the comic antics of these three comedians.

For more of the American antique influence watch Orson Wells in *Citizen Kane,* particularly his love for his old sled, "Rosebud", which Kane cherished throughout his life. Many of us had a sled of our own. For some more interesting antique scenery was *Auntie Mame* with Rosalind Russell and *The Music Man* with Robert Preston. Another movie with a lot of flash, color and antique settings is *Oklahoma* with Shirley Jones and Gordon McRae.

We recently watched *The Human Comedy* starring Ralph Morgan and Mickey Rooney, adapted from a novel by William Saroyan. While only about fifty years old, there are some good shots of old telegraph equipment, small town newspaper equipment, and the old railway stations and steam locomotives. For more nostalgia see *The Great Gatsby,* an F. Scott Fitzgerald story starring Robert Redford which highlights the manners, clothing, and decor of the "jazz age". All this sounds like a movie review but it is a good itinerary of antique research. They provoke comments from the viewers such as, "Boy! Would I like to have that floor lamp!", or "Now, that's the way a booth should be set up to look like a typical room in an old home."

One type of old movie I watch takes me out of the realm of antique research. These are the old Mae West films. When my wife says, "Look at that old wicker chair!", I say, "You look at what you like and I'll look at what I like!"

MANAGEMENT—A NEW BALL OF TWINE

The managers of our complex had been supervising it for twelve years. I imagine we did things the way they wanted them done as we didn't see much of them, except on rent payment days. The lady manager was very helpful to us when we entered the antique world and was willing to share a lot of her knowledge of this business. Her greatest worry seemed to be the public restroom located in the complex. There wasn't much activity around the place during the weekdays but she always drove around the building at least once a day and checked to make sure the restroom door was locked. I was generally there, working at something, and sometimes was the only dealer on the premises. When she didn't make daily rounds, she always called me to "check out" the restroom, knowing I was usually there. Her concern and obsession with the restroom puzzled me.

The only problem I ever had with her husband was over a TV antenna my son and I had erected on the roof. A football fan, I was not satisfied with the reception we were receiving with only the "rabbit ears". After we had spent considerable time putting it up there, he made us take it down, reminding me of the great cost of a new roof the owners were still paying for and stated, "We don't want people walking around up there, punching holes through it." He didn't like my cat either, but didn't press on that matter. Other than that, I had the impression that they had an easy job of managing or that they made the job *look* easy. Two years later the man became seriously ill and remained so for some time. When he passed away, his wife lost interest in the business and sold her share of the complex to my wife and me. The remaining partners encouraged us to take up the managership. Our only compensation would be reduced rent for our shop but having formed an opinion that the job was "a piece of cake", we accepted the responsibility.

My wife and fellow dealers advised me that my first project as manager should be, strangely enough, to refurbish the public restroom. "It's dirty, needs painting, also needs a place for people to sit while they're waiting and could use a better rug", my wife advised. I received other recommendations from other dealers such as, "It should be cleaned more often", or "The place is too cold in winter", and "the least you could do would be to paint over those awful 'outhouse etchings'". I could now visualize that after all these tasks had been accomplished, I might have a fixation on the restroom as strong as my predecessor.

My daughter and I painted, cleaned the restroom and waiting room, hung some cheap but attractive pictures and put down a new rug; well, at least a better one that had been there. We even provided a small table and some antique literature to read for those waiting their turn. We also placed a mirror in the restroom to cover a hole in the wall and installed a globe over one lone light bulb. It was downright beautiful! After all our efforts, my advisors now told me, "Don't make it too nice or the customers will tear it up!" We were beginning to get both sides of the management equation just from trying to "shape up the powder room".

My wife, daughter and I developed an aversion to cleaning the place up after awhile and looked for help. One of the dealers said she knew a young girl who lived on a farm across the highway who would clean the restroom for a meager sum. She reported to me one day and I instructed her as to the areas to be cleaned. She walked out of the back door of the shop and was back in ten minutes, stating "I'm done. There wasn't much to do." It was true that there wasn't much to do as she had done nothing. This would start a long and generally unsuccessful search for a restroom cleaner; my first trial as the new manager.

Another lady, one of the most successful dealers, told me, "You and your daughter did a fine job of fixing up that restroom, but you forgot one thing." "What might that be?", I asked. "You forgot to wash the windows in the waiting room", she added. Off I went again, armed with my cleaning cloth and Windex bottle.

Several days later, one of my dealer's prediction about vandalism proved to be correct. "The outhouse poet has struck again", he informed me. Well, my daughter and I refused to let anyone destroy the results of our hard work. We would cover the culprit's work with some paint we had saved. Let him write himself silly! The author of our problem persisted and I finally applied the remedy of a friend of mine who operated a saloon. I installed a blackboard, equipped with chalk and eraser in the restroom. It worked!

With this challenge overcome, things seemed to get better. Another dealer's daughter came to me and announced she would clean the waiting room and restroom for a nominal fee. She did turn out to be reliable and with this "thorn in my side" removed, I could address the next project.

There was an overall peculiar circumstance existing in this old motel building. Being a motel, all the rooms had a "powder room" and when converted to shops, each shop had a toilet; however, only half of them functioned. We used to refer to the complex as the half and half structure; the half we loved and the half we hated. From the middle shop, which was ours, to the North end of the structure, the toilets worked but those to the South did not. After making a number of inquiries about the matter, we learned a previous manager had become angry with a dealer for non-payment of rent; subsequently he armed himself with a sledge hammer and broke the main sewage line to the shop. In doing so, he cut off all the shops instead of just one. We located a plumber who surveyed the problem and submitted a reasonable estimate of cost to correct the situation. The owners approved the estimate and the project was completed. Now our dealer friends to the South, all had working toilets and happiness prevailed as they flushed merrily.

Why should restrooms and their associated problems require the attention of an entire vignette? This question puzzled me until I talked with managers of other business enterprises. Regardless of the nature of their business, restroom maintenance seemed to require a lot of time and caused more trouble than any other facet of management. One manager told me, "Bookkeeping is a 'snap' compared to operating a good restroom".

Things went well until mid-February when winter truly descended upon us. All my illusions of "smooth sailing" were shattered when, one morning, a customer entered the shop and brought the sad tidings, "Your toilet in your restroom is froze up". My toilet? My restroom? Why me?? Ah, the challenge of management.

MANAGEMENT AND ADVERTISING—MORE EDUCATION

Just about the time we had the maintenance of our complex under control, advertising reared its ugly head. When we assumed our new role of managers, we were totally "in the dark" as to another facet of management called advertising. It came up like the dawn in a thunderous manner, to steal a line from Kipling. We did know that each month, at the same time we paid our rent, we also contributed a small fee for advertising which the managers used at their discretion. The sum of the fee was based on the size of the shop and the number of rooms rented. None of the fees exceeded twenty dollars.

The previous managers tired of doing it and turned it over to my neighboring dealer and his partner who were responsible for advertising when my wife and I assumed managership. Their approach was very simple as they used small ads in the local newspapers and some handbills to be passed out to customers or at antique shows. Occasionally they would run some information in the large, big-city newspaper of our area. After one such expenditure of funds, a number of the dealers came to me, not too gently either, about the high cost of advertising in the big-city publication and its relative value to our business. "In that paper", one dealer said, "the ad is so small nobody would even see it, much less read it! Why don't you do something about it?" I suggested they talk to the dealers responsible for advertising. Another dealer told me, "We did and just made them mad and they did the same thing again!"

Like a fool, I approached these partners with a certain degree of confidence, as we had been neighbors for so long. Adaline and I were certain we could influence them to try some new techniques. We saw them sitting outside their shop on the following day and made our approach. I opened my dumb mouth first by saying, "Some of the dealers came to me complaining about advertising, wanting some new approaches and ideas and suggested we talk with you and see if we could be of any help." "You can", the one partner said, "could you wait here just a minute?" He entered their shop, returned and presented the advertising account to my wife and I. "This is how you can help", he said, "take it; it is now yours." "But we just wanted to talk about it", my wife said. "The talk is over!", was his only reply. The other partner just sat there, nodding his head. It reminded me of a Bartles and James commercial.

We informed the other dealers that we had just inherited the advertising account and decided on a democratic approach to the problem by calling a meeting of all of them in order to hear new ideas. To further the cause of uniting all the complainers in one location, we also thought it would be well to have them bring some beverage and snacks; we would have the meeting on Saturday evening, after closing time; a brilliant idea we thought at the time.

The meeting was well attended with only two dealers absent and they had passed the word they would be in agreement with the decisions that were made. We began, libation in hand, munching on potato chips, etc. I started by announcing that the advertising account had been summarily placed in our hands by the previous administrators; then I read the current status of the account. Judging from the balance on hand, it didn't take a genius long to figure out that not much advertising had been done recently or for the last few months for that matter. "You see!", one woman dealer blurted out, "they haven't done a thing! They were fiddling with our money!" "Fiddle with yourself", the previous advertising agent said as the silent partner nodded in agreement. Then they left the meeting.

After this short disagreement and interruption, one of the dealers recommended a special event near the first of each month to attract customers. One would take place during the current month, September, and continue on until Christmas. The events would take place as follows: September—each shop would give a door prize; October—each dealer would move some merchandise to the sidewalk outside and provide an indoor-outdoor atmosphere; November—each dealer to have an open house with refreshments in their shops; December—each shop to offer free gifts to children and the shops to be appropriately decorated. This met with overall approval and the meeting slowly diminished to friendly conversation and then to a rather well developed party.

We had, at least, performed one service to the complex. The dealers began to talk to each other instead of *about* each other. We placed the announcement of these events in the local newspapers and in the surrounding military bases' newspapers and bulletins. Most of the dealers cooperated with the plan of events but the results were negligible. Then the dealers came to us with comments such as, "These events took too much time for the results we get!" We would remind them, "Well, you all created the plan and agreed to go ahead with it".

So far, we had covered our tracks to perfection. We tried some other methods such as TV "blurbs" and radio, etc. One of the humorous things that happened was the result of a planned general "open house" in the spring of the year. One of the dealers had taken it upon himself to purchase a large balloon to fly over the complex and attract attention. The first exciting event of the open house was generated by a child who had found a pair of scissors someplace and cut the retaining cord of the balloon. The balloon could be seen later in the day, floating beautifully and at great height over the Chesapeake Bay.

The dealers began to arrive on our doorstep again. One said, "That was dumb, letting that guy spend all that money on a silly balloon when it could have been used for some sensible advertising." Another said, "I heard you spent money for flowers for one of the dealers who was in the hospital. This is an advertising account; not a benevolence account!" "This is now your account", I replied, "You receive it as I received it. Good luck and be sure to invite us to your next meeting!" He lasted a couple of months, then another victim a couple of months, and so on as we kept trying to solve the advertising puzzle. One good thing came of it. The meetings continued to turn into parties and the parties grew better. We could have done much worse.

MANAGEMENT AND MAINTENANCE

Having survived the restroom and advertising problems, we saw other elements of management on the horizon coming to torment us. These had to do with collecting rent, general maintenance and security problems that arose. Maintenance problems in the past had been handled by the handyman and those things that went wrong that he could not correct were simply dismissed and forgotten. This approach does cut down on expenses. Collecting rent at this time was not a problem as the rent had remained constant for about ten years. The correction of maintenance problems ran parallel to rent collection; nothing changed. Security was provided by a bachelor Office from the Sheriff's Department who was furnished a rent free apartment for his services. This apartment consisted of a small kitchen, living room, bedroom and a shower room. Some of the kitchen equipment did not work, the shower leaked, the refrigerator would not defrost and the heating was marginal. These discrepancies had been of long standing. On the security side of the coin, the officer was absent many nights due to his duties with the Sheriff's Office.

Another security problem was adequate lighting. This old motel building had peripheral lighting at one time that functioned very well but now only four lights, two in back of the building and two in front were working, and these tended to cast more shadows than provide light. Soon the dealers arrived on our threshold complaining about these deficiencies. Their complaints about lighting in the past had fallen on deaf ears. One fellow dealer advised us. "With good lights here, we could stay open later at night. WE would all benefit from good lighting."

With that thought in mind, we pressed on. About the time the lighting problem was addressed, we thought of two other items to which we should direct our attention; rewiring the building and providing air-conditioning. A used appliance dealer in Virginia offered these items with both air-conditioning and heating capabilities for a sensible cost. The dealer, who had his own maintenance shop, guaranteed them for one year. The dealers agreed to buy their own units provided the owners' installed the necessary power lines. This we did and also corrected some faulty circuits in the building as well. Previously, if just one extra fixture was plugged into some of the circuits, it would overload and four or five shops would be without power until it was repaired. We could always tell when this happened, because we could see the dealers coming down the sidewalk with determined looks in their eyes. This fault we corrected as well, as illuminating a large sign out front and placing spotlights on all the shops. These were controlled by timers which activated the lights at dusk and shut off about nine o'clock. Man, it was beautiful!

The owners of the complex agreed on the improvements and their high cost with the stipulation that the rents be raised. The dealers were as happy as "dogs with three tails" with the improvements but "thunder and lightning" struck when the rents were adjusted. In my estimation, the "lightning" would have illuminated Baltimore for a night or two. "That rent is ridiculous!", one dealer announced. He had been heard previously, condemning our lighting deficiencies. My only comment was, "Go up the road six miles and you can pay twice the rent you're paying here. We don't even charge you for electricity but they will up the road!" He did not move up the road.

Things were going along very nicely when one of the owners called my wife and reported, "We just happened to be driving by the complex, returning from a trip South, and noticed the lights were still on at three o'clock in the morning. You really don't need lights all night do you?" I had set the timer wrong. After this was corrected, we had no further problems. The interesting part of this whole process was that the dealers lost interest in staying in the shops after dark. The general observation was, "We didn't notice that much difference in the amount of sales." It was, however, a good move toward better security and none could deny that fact.

"Well, we've just about put this place in good shape", my wife commented. About that time I had another brainstorm. Our trash disposal people had not been doing a very good job. They would unload the dumpster into their truck but the remainder left on the ground would remain there until we picked it up. We had a friend in this business and decided to hire him and discontinue the contract with the other agent. The dumpster was removed and replaced by a string of fifty-five gallon cans provided by our friend in front of each shop. We painted them green and they had a better appearance than the dumpster plus serving their basic purpose very well; for awhile. Then an event we hadn't counted on took place. Every vacationing group, whether traveling by car, motorcycle, trailer or camper stopped by to say "Hello" and also fill our trash cans. Did I say fill? I meant fill to overflowing. Here came the parade of dealers again, complaining, "The highway is full of trash bins but they stop and use ours. They don't buy anything either!" We reverted back to the dumpster, but this time in the rear of the building. We were beginning to see that trash disposal was cyclical, dumpster to trash can to dumpster, etc.

We slowly started to approach an overall improvement era when the roof started to leak again. The roof was practically new but during a period of very hot weather, the sealer in some of the seams melted. Now, you would think it would be easy to find someone who could correct this type of problem but we had a terrible time finding a man who could do the work properly. Finally, this was accomplished and we fooled ourselves with the idea that we could now take a "breather".

The final job was to have our sidewalks repaired and the "pot holes" on our perimeter road filled. Our insurance representative would not renew our policy if we didn't complete these repairs. We were rewarded for all our efforts by the smiles on the dealers' faces. Then the place was practically damaged by two bad fires. After the fires and the fireman had done what they had to do, you could look through the place from front to back. Talk about a maintenance problem! "Well, we'll have to put up a new sign", I told my wife. It would read, *OUR BUSINESS IS MORE OPEN THAN USUAL TODAY.* "Not funny today", she replied. She also continued to accuse me of being "flippant" about the fire. I don't feel "flippant" at all. We lost an interesting business and a lot of customers and dealers, friends all; not in business, we don't see as much of them as we like. We worked very hard to improve the complex for all concerned and now it is no more.

A BRIEF SAYONARA—NO MORE PLAYING HOUSE

I suppose since my wife and I, while never poor, grew up watching some of our contemporaries live in, what we styled, as luxury, the antique world opened a door to a second home, filled with beautiful paintings, furniture, and items representing man's skillful interpretation of life as he saw it down through the decades. What we sold—fine! What we didn't sell is in our home; these items would be a compliment to any antique lover's home.

Some days, having other commitments, we would say, "How will we split the day? Do you want to go to the shop early or should I?" Many times Adaline would say, "Do what you have to do and I'll play house today. I like to play house!" Our shop rooms and booths at shows looked like room settings. Many people complimented us on this. Sometimes, I think my wife would have liked to have been an interior decorator. Her arrangements were always superb.

Everything wears out. Now we look to fishing, traveling, going to shows as customers, and golf. We truthfully didn't make a lot of money in the antique world. There's no more "playing house", but other things remain. The memories of new friends; these are promoters, dealers, (like the guy who always helped me when he thought I was lifting too much), and customers alike, whose conversation was sometimes more uplifting than a sale, we retain from the antique world.

Salute!

Our shop after the devastating fire.